FAITH HOPE LOVE

The Essentials of Christianity for the
Curious, Confused, and Skeptical

Colin Kerr

ISBN: 978-1-0878-1836-8

Printed in the United States of America.

special thanks

———————●———————

To my biblical research assistant, Morgan Byars,
and to my seminary professor, Dr. Susan Forshey.

And to the atheist, agnostic, and spiritually exploring friends
and students who provided critical feedback,
Gabi Loue, Aaron Allsbrook, Katie Kurtz, Allie Stern, Robin Loucks,
Sarah Elizabeth, Duncan Kackley, Rebecca Simmons, Charlotte Cooper,
Elizabeth Simons and Jordan Harrison.

This book is dedicated to my daughter, Arland.

Table of Contents

INTRODUCTION
The Reason

You think it would be easy.

Defining what it means to be a Christian *should* be easy on the face of it. We live in the modern Western world. In our culture Christianity is the prevailing religion. There is not a town with a stoplight without a church in it. Many politicians even claim the United States is a Christian nation.

So why is it so difficult to define what it means to be a Christian? Ask someone who identifies as a Christian, and you'll get as many different answers as asking someone who isn't – probably more. For as much as non-Christians may struggle to understand what Christianity is, Christians have added to the confusion.

There are dozens of major Christian denominations and thousands of minor denominations – some a denomination of a single church. While not all will give you different definitions of Christianity, many will.

"That denomination or church isn't teaching *true* Christianity," they will say, "*We* are."

I used to think that this problem of defining the heart of Christianity was confined to tiny, backwoods churches with grandiose names. A lack of education and an abundance of hubris can cause the kind of religious pride that makes a person think they have the only true version of Christianity. When I tried to find a concise book on the essentials of Christian beliefs, even otherwise cultured and prominent theologians got caught up conflating their personal beliefs with *true* Christianity.

I read a book from a mega-church pastor who claimed he wanted to give the most basic and explicit beliefs of Christianity. I was shocked to discover that one of his essential tenets of the Christian faith included rejecting the theory of evolution. *True* Christianity, he said, required a belief in some form of creationism. Otherwise, you weren't *really* believing in Christianity, but instead some watered-down knockoff version.

What Essential Christianity is Not

That mega-church pastor wasn't alone in this line of thinking. There are all sorts of Christians who will tell you that in order to be a Christian, you must hold to the same essential beliefs as them. This might be fair enough if these essential beliefs were limited to a short list. Yet what is so frustrating is that many Christians are unable to distinguish between essential beliefs for *all* Christians and non-essential beliefs that one may feel strongly about as an *individual* Christian. So before we can even begin talking about what essential Christianity is, it's important to acknowledge what it is not.

Like that mega-church pastor, more conservative Christians might declare that you *must* believe in an eternity of conscious torment in Hell for non-Christians. You *must* believe that same-sex marriage is evil and threatens to ruin the country. You *must* believe in taking the Bible literally – except when Jesus tells his followers to pluck out their eyeballs and cut off their hands if they cause them to sin. I've never seen anyone who believes taking the Bible literally preach self-amputation. Literal interpretations, even for very conservative Christians, have their limits.

It's not just more conservative Christians though. More liberal or progressive[1] Christians might announce that you *must* believe in supporting all forms of social justice. You *must* believe capitalism is evil and threatens to ruin our country. You *must* believe that sincere people of all faiths have access to God – except suicidal cults and religiously-inspired terrorists. Tolerance and inclusion, even for very progressive Christians, have their limits.

I don't mean to sound flippant. These issues, whether about justice, sexuality, other religions, or the best way to interpret the Bible are important questions that faithful Christians have intensely debated in the past and will continue to debate in the future. However, these kind of issues have not and never will be part of the essential beliefs of historical Christianity.

No person should ever feel that central to becoming a follower of Christ, they must follow a particular political agenda. No person should ever feel that central to entering into a relationship with God, they must reject – or accept – evolution, same-sex marriage, or a particular fate for the billions of people who will never hear about the message of Christianity.

---

[1] Theologically and/or politically liberal Christians generally prefer the term "progressive," which itself can be confusing since a politically liberal Christian and a theologically liberal Christian are not one in the same. Since 2016 in the United States, a similar distinction has emerged among the "conservative" Christian label.

Let me be clear. I think Christians should faithfully discern their views on those things as part of a deepening faith. Christianity is meant to speak to the entirety of the human experience. Yet we must be very careful in not declaring anything more than the most essential of things as the heart of Christianity. Christians, I confess, have not often exercised that thoughtful caution, which has led to a heartbreaking amount of confusion.

The Decline of "Imperial" Christianity

These mixed messages have been made worse by an anxiety about the slow death of institutional Christianity in the United States.

All the surveys, polling, and demographic data paint a grim picture of a religion that has seen its best years come and go. In the twentieth century, Europe saw its Christian religion disintegrate into a shell of its former glory as abandoned churches littered the landscape. Most commentators today, even many pastors and ministers, expect that while Christianity in the United States will not decline as much as it did in Europe, the twenty-first century will herald irreversible losses. This loss of institutional prestige, and the evaporation of the political power that often accompanied it, has created unprecedented fear in the hearts of many Christian leaders.

As you may have noticed, this has caused some Christians then to behave rather "un-Christian." Ugly culture wars are waged against imaginary boogeymen, typically in opposition to people that didn't vote, worship, or live like those Christians thought they should. Never mind that these were people wondrously made and loved by God. Too many Christian leaders were anxious about their continued influence. They saw demons where they should have seen friends, and saw friends where they should have been

4

exorcising their own personal demons of power and control. Every election cycle feels like a new demonstration that institutional Christianity is more than willing to betray its alleged values, and non-Christians have not missed the rank hypocrisy. Christianity, at least on a national level in the United States, seems to stand for very little these days other than justifying a feeling of moral superiority for predetermined partisan platforms and clawing for scraps of political privilege. Even the scraps, I imagine, will soon be taken from us.

Perhaps this was long overdue. Perhaps this was inevitable.

Amazingly, Jesus of Nazareth – the person Christians believe was God incarnate – predicted that his movement of a handful of poor, mostly illiterate peasants scraping by in a backwater province under the bloody heel of an oppressive empire would somehow explode out "to the ends of the earth." It is an historical phenomenon that defies satisfactory explanation.

Yet Jesus never taught that his movement should become the controlling force in politics and culture, wielding the levers of power and coercion to remake the remaining world in its religious vision. As we'll later explore, Jesus talked about something called *the Kingdom of God*, but he never hinted at what could be construed as an empire of Christian religion. In this Kingdom of God, the followers of Jesus were meant to be humble and spiritual, not domineering and institutional.

You might be confused then why Christianity at times seems to act opposite to its founder's values. Unfortunately, human nature, full of mixed motives and an insatiable desire for control, could account for most of this poor behavior. A strange turn in history, which inadvertently magnified these downsides of human nature, might explain the rest.

Christianity's shocking fourth-century triumph over the Roman Empire and its subsequent fifth-century adoption as the Roman religion by politically savvy emperors transformed Christianity from a faith on the political margins to a religion of institutional power. Christianity was never really comfortable dressed in imperial purple and golden laurels, but somehow found itself coronated in an ancient world that necessitated a singular uniting religion to establish political legitimacy. It's hard to overstate the impact this had on the dynamic of Christianity, once religious doctrine became entangled with the power of the state. The Kingdom kind of Christianity was gradually replaced in most places with the "imperial" kind of Christianity.

So perhaps this imperial and coercive strain of Christianity that has been most common[2] ever since Emperor Constantine's successors declared that strange cult of Christ worshipers as the religion of the State, is finally dying because it was never endorsed by Christ in the first place. The Kingdom of God, as Jesus promises, would never see "the gates of Hell prevail against it." The empire of Christianity, however, may very well be a blip in the history of humanity.

The Return of Kingdom Christianity

This is not to say that these two versions of Christianity have had fundamentally different beliefs. Imperial or institutional Christianity inherited an unshakeable theological core from Kingdom Christianity. They are both the same Christianity in that sense. The difference is less about belief systems and more about a posture – pride and power or humility and relationship. Today, imperial Christianity is identified more by what it stands against. Kingdom

---

[2] There are plenty of exceptions throughout history worth exploring (such as some monastic traditions or the Anabaptists), but they have existed as minority expressions of Christianity.

Christianity has always been identified more by what it stood for.

A number of atheists and agnostics[3] who helped to edit this book said to me something to the effect of, "I really like this explanation of Christianity, but is this *actually* Christianity?" Discussing it more, I discovered that they wondered if I wasn't just offering some new version of Christianity that hadn't yet existed. What they were really sensing though, I believe, was a difference in the posture from the more pervasive institutional Christianity they previously had encountered.

If the imperial or institutional kind of Christianity is slowly dying in the West,[4] there is new room for the Kingdom kind of Christianity to return. With this transition are new opportunities, not for a new version of Christianity molded to modern fads, but a version more faithful to the spirit and attitude of its earliest pre-imperial expressions. In the meantime, many people will be understandably curious, confused, or skeptical about what it means to be a Christian. Some may even be rightly skeptical of the imperial kind of Christianity, unaware there is a Kingdom of God hidden among the margins.

That is a central reason for this book: to affirm that your rejection of imperial Christianity may not be the terrible offense some Christians have made it out to be. In fact, your reasons for rejecting institutional Christianity might have – unbeknownst to you – been more faithful to the nature of Kingdom Christianity than some claiming to be Christian themselves. This may seem counterintuitive, but the idea that those who are condemned by stodgy, religious people are

---

[3] A-theism = no-God. A-gnosticism = no-knowledge. "Agnostic" refers to those who accept the possibility of God, but are not convinced either.

[4] The better theories range from the internet creating new access to religious and philosophical information to blowback from Christians aligning with right-wing politics.

actually closer to the way of God is a theme that comes up again and again in the origins of the Christian movement.[5]

Who Is This Book For?

This, admittedly, is a peculiar book. It's hard to place it in a neat category. In one sense, this is for those who are simply curious about the basic beliefs of the Christian faith and wish to become more informed. In another sense, this is also for those who have grown up in a church, but are now confused if what they were taught growing up was as universally embraced by other Christians as they were led to believe. Still, my heart cannot forget the skeptic, a label that even as a minister I identify with to this day. As I have been at different seasons in my life and with different struggles regarding the Christian faith, this is for the skeptic who is open to considering (or reconsidering) Christianity while wishing to avoid being debated into Christianity. Whether you are curious, confused, or skeptical, this book is meant to clear the air and then clear up some issues.

Maybe you've heard that to be a Christian, you need to just be a relatively good person who believes in God, which in your more introspective moments makes you curious as to what the big fuss about Christianity is anyway. After all, there are plenty of people not going to church that are doing a much better job at being nice and kind than people you'll see in the pews every Sunday. What exactly does this Christian religion believe, and does this first-century faith from the Middle East have any relevance in my twenty-first-century life, racked with both unprecedented technological progress and social upheaval?

Maybe after witnessing all the behavior that seems so unlike the Jesus his followers claim to represent, you are

---

[5] Luke 10:25-37; Luke 18:9-14

confused about what exactly a Christian is. Perhaps you've heard that to be a Christian, you need to buy into this laundry list of detailed religious beliefs, many of which you have serious reservations about. Is it really reasonable to believe that your relationship with a possible God and the meaning of your life hangs on your thoughts about something like a cosmic big bang or a virgin giving birth?

Maybe this whole religion thing, regardless of what religion we're talking about, seems a bit like a moral and intellectual straightjacket. Sure, it's helpful for those who need that kind of structure in their lives, but you're skeptical that the Christian faith can be any different than any other world religion that offers salvation in exchange for you giving up your personal freedom. Are there any good reasons to believe Christianity is actually true, and that it's not just another pyramid scheme for gullible people who struggle to think for themselves?

What then is the heart of the Christian faith, and why – in spite of all the ugly messes some Christians have made – is it worth considering? If you are curious, confused, or skeptical about the essential beliefs of Christianity, my hope is simply to offer whatever clarity is necessary.

The rest is between you and God.

FAITH HOPE LOVE

CHAPTER ONE
The Wager

Disclaimer: I am not interested in arguing you into believing Christianity. Despite studying philosophy in college under all atheist professors and receiving a Master of Divinity through a faithful little Presbyterian seminary – where I debated theology with my professors over beers – I've never seen someone argued into becoming a follower of Jesus.

It's not that Christian faith is irrational, but there has always seemed to be something about the way of Jesus that only became rational once one took their first step in trusting this Jesus.[6] Søren Kierkegaard, the nineteenth century Danish philosopher and founder of existentialism,[7] characterized it as a leap made by faith out of the illusions of self-reliance and

---

[6] 1 Corinthians 1:18
[7] An assortment of philosophies that all wrestle with discomfort of human existence and stresses its problematic character of personal choice and uncertainty.

"pure" reason. One of Jesus's disciples, Peter, is recorded in the Bible as experiencing the abstractions of Kierkegaard in a more visceral way. Jesus told him to get out of the boat and onto a raging sea. Walking on water might seem like a terribly irrational idea in and of itself, but after taking your first two steps because Jesus asked you to, suddenly it seems quite rational to keep your eyes fixed on the One who is standing upon the water with you.[8]

Faith, as understood by Christianity, is neither fundamentally rational nor irrational, but relational. Why relational? All relationships require some evidence to authenticate themselves, but no healthy relationship survives off a constant demand for evidence. Faith, understood in this way, is not blind faith. Only once trust is established, it is a kind of faith that has the power to endure through perceived droughts of evidence.

I am also not interested in defending Christianity. If you've come looking for a combative debate or for exhaustive apologetics, non-Christian and Christian alike, you probably will be disappointed. You'll find that I actually tend to agree with most common critiques of institutional Christianity. This isn't to say intellectually robust defenses of Christianity for dispelling misinformation or proving the historical reliability of the biblical texts don't have their place, but I like what the nineteenth-century British theologian Charles Spurgeon said: "Open the door and let the lion out; he will take care of himself." If Christianity is indeed the way to encounter God most fully, and if God is anything like a lion, I trust God can defend Godself. God doesn't need me to come to God's rescue.

During the earthly life of Jesus, every time someone asked him to defend his teachings with a miraculous sign, he flatly refused.[9] Far from endless debates, his confrontations

---

[8] Matthew 14:22-33
[9] Matthew 12:39

with the religious elites were also surprisingly brief. After the death and resurrection of Jesus, his disciples-turned-apostles (literally *messengers*) found the truth was more than capable of defending itself. No less dramatic than the Roman spear that pierced a deceased Jesus on the cross, the first Christian sermon proclaimed by the apostle Peter "pierced the heart" of his skeptical audience.[10]

I believe that the Christian message we will encounter in these coming chapters, when clearly grasped as much as it is clearly articulated, will create an internally powerful reaction within the receiver. Biblical stories and human history demonstrate that this reaction will be either acceptance, rejection, or intense curiosity. These same stories and history do not, however, indicate I am capable of determining which reaction you will choose. My responsibility, at least in these pages, is simply to provide a sufficient explanation of the Christian faith that you can accept, reject, or resolve to investigate further with accurate understanding.

A Fair Wager

Why, though, bother at all? Perhaps you are truly curious about understanding the essential heart of the Christian faith so you can wrestle with whether it's reasonable to consider forming your life around it. You might be a spiritually discerning person like that, and if so, you are in a minority.

Long-term data shows American culture is almost as spiritually interested as it was a hundred years ago,[11] but our spiritual interest has mutated from a communal faith to an individualized consumer religion.[12] The focus on truth of a

---

[10] John 19:34; Acts 2:37
[11] David Briggs, "Is Religion In America In Decline?" *The Huffington Post*, June 2, 2011.
[12] Michael Lipka, "5 Key Findings about Religiosity in the U.S. – and How It's Changing," Pew Research Center, November 03, 2015.

spiritual nature has moved from objective and sacrificial to subjective and therapeutic.

A consequence of modern consumer culture, a rapidly growing number of people form their spiritual beliefs not necessarily on what they believe is true, but on what is most functionally helpful for their life at any given moment. If some spirituality, meditation, or crystal can be harnessed for a better sense of well-being, then it becomes "true" for that particular person – which is usually all that really matters as far as they're concerned. For an increasing number of people today, utility is truth and truth is utility.

So why exert the effort to consider a Christian faith whose founder advertised it by announcing to the crowds who had come to hear him, "Whoever wants to be my disciple must deny themself and take up their cross daily and follow me. For whoever wants to save their life will lose it, but whoever loses their life for me will save it"?[13] Despite what you have heard or seen to the contrary in the Western world, Christianity is not the easiest of the world's faiths. Instead of being personally useful, Christianity often makes daily life for its adherents very inconvenient. Why sign up for that?

Blaise Pascal, a brilliant French scientist in the seventeenth century and a convert to Christianity from the religious nominalism of his day, wrote in an unfinished work that God, while not irrational, was ultimately beyond rationality. Since the existence of God could not be proven nor disproven, the skeptic should then believe in God on the basis of a heavenly reward. If you follow God and God is real, you get Heaven. If you follow God and God is not real, you suffer no real loss.

This is an oversimplified version of Pascal's logic, but the crudity of reducing faith to a cosmic game of roulette has

---

[13] Matthew 16:24

been debunked by skeptics and believers alike. It is not considered the best argument for Christianity by anyone. Even still, "Pascal's Wager," as it has come to be known, does present a good point. The wager can't logically or ethically cajole us into faith, but it can prompt us to consider the possibilities of it. What compelling reason is there to expend the time and effort in weighing the claims of the Christian faith?

Mercenary vs. Revolutionary

You might think this is the part where I tell you Christianity is worth considering because you would hate to miss out on eternal bliss in Heaven. No. We should consider the Christian faith not because of the afterlife, but because of this life. If the heart of Christianity is indeed true – not just for you or me, but for the whole world – such a reality has the power to change the world in a way no other philosophy, ideology, or religion can. It will still reverberate into eternity, but this eternity need not be delayed to some distant point on humanity's horizon or in the sweet by-and-by of Heaven. The world is meant to be changed, not later, but now.

Considering Christianity only to secure your place in Heaven is mercenary. Considering Christianity to partner with God to heal the world is revolutionary. The wager I hope you will be willing to make is not a mercenary one. Rather, it would be a revolutionary willingness to consider a covert reality veiled beyond what is normally seen, and a purpose hidden from us in plain sight.

If Christianity might be true, and the reason to consider it is not about getting to Heaven but instead bringing pieces of Heaven to earth, what exactly are these pieces? How can the Christian faith, the Kingdom kind that exploded across the ancient world as a grassroots movement, revolutionize and revitalize our understanding of reality?

I suggest there are five major ways in which Christianity can radically change your life: your purpose, your story, your identity, your perseverance, and your ethics. We'll explore these now individually and then in greater detail later on in corresponding chapters.

Purpose

All religions offer their adherents purpose for their lives, some kind of assurance that their existence is not merely an accident of indifferent colliding atoms. When we reflect on life's greatest joys and our greatest pains, most people want to find comfort in the knowledge that there was some deeper meaning to them. The birth of a child is more than just our evolutionary impulses successfully propagating our genetic material. The unexpected death of a loved one is more than an annihilation of that similar genetic material from which there will never be recompense.

In between those highs and lows, most people want to feel like what they're doing counts for *something*. No one, not even the nihilist who claims life is pointless, finds deep enjoyment pondering the possibility that everything they've ever done, including simply existing, will be utterly forgotten after enough time. I want a significance, if but even in a small way, that will extend beyond my death and the world's memory of my life. Most religions to some degree offer an encouraging answer to this fundamental human need for purpose.

It should come as no surprise that the Christian faith does as well. However, what I hope you find about Christianity is that our purpose demands everything of a person without constraining them to a narrow path of choices. This is a balance rarely struck in most faiths or individualistic spiritualities.

In major faiths of the world, the devoutly religious tend to form strict expectations about behavior, often codifying those expectations into religious rules. The purpose might be clear, even nobly sacrificial, but it stifles personal creativity and deadens critical thinking. Followers submit to what a given religion claims to be true even if it doesn't seem to actually "work" in the face of the complexities of daily life. Meanwhile, the individualistically spiritual who often believe in something like a "higher power," tend to enjoy the flexibility of defining their own purpose. They are often more open to new ideas and inclusive of others, but eventually that same subjectivity means they cannot escape how they measure their spiritual "success" without also evaluating their own personal happiness. Instead of trying to pursue what is really true, they pursue what feels best. All experiences, even the people they know, eventually become the means to an end by which the individualistically spiritual gratify an inwardly focused purpose.

Christian purpose is meant to be both all-encompassing and liberating. It undermines a person's sense of entitlement to gratification, but also provides an opportunity for liberation from the straightjacket of merciless black-and-white dogma. This purpose lived out produces an indwelling state of being that allows a person to experience a kind of happiness that is not contingent on positive circumstances.

Though this sense of well-being is not unique to Christianity, Christians have uniquely called this kind of enduring happiness *joy*.

Story

All people, religious or irreligious, agree this world isn't perfect. In fact, such a description is terribly understated. The world can be profoundly tragic and cruel. It can also be awe-inspiring and moving. The worst and best seem to play out daily in economics, politics, the sciences, media, and even our friendships.

What narrative best makes sense of how the world is, why it became that way, and where it is going? Is there a fundamental problem that plagues the human experience, and if there is, can there be a solution? Here too, many religions will offer different explanations, some more plausible than others. My hope is that you'll see the story that Christians believe God is writing not as a cliché moralistic fable, but rather a grand narrative worthy of its cosmic proportions.

Yet a happy story does not make it a true story. Pie-in-the-sky religion is ultimately selfish and embarrassing. However, while much of the Christian faith anticipates the possibility of redemption for human nature and our dilemmas, I believe it can also provide realistic and steely-eyed explanatory powers that allow us to see through the competing secular narratives given to us by those same corporations, politicians, scientists, media pundits, and even our friends. The promise of the Christian story is that it invites us to see the world not as an unending quest for comfort, or "red in tooth and claw" Darwinism, nor as a story dominated by power plays and written by the oppressors who claim their rule will be eternal, but as a divine narrative that ties all ancient hopes together and exposes the myths of the oppressors.

It's a story that is not written *by* us, but written *for* us.

Identity

Who are you? No, not your name. Who. Are. You? This seemingly innocuous question can become bewildering as soon as we begin to think about all that is wrapped up in it.

Your identity speaks to your sense of personal worth.[14] Your identity reveals where your deepest loyalties lie. Your identity points you back to your true self. Your identity is the incredible depth of who you are, right underneath the surface of your name.

Just as we were named by someone else at our birth, our identity is foisted on us as well. The only difference is that we can choose which of those identities we want to internalize in our psyches. There are a thousand identities peddled and pushed on us. Identities that are healthy and those that wreck us. Identities that inspire us and those that shame us. Identities that bring us into harmony with reality and those that trick us into chasing mirages.

Every one of us, within our lifetime, will try on dozens of different identities. They are not fixed or permanent. While some identities are harmonious, in that they overlap and reinforce one another, many are competing. Christianity teaches your core identity, the one that acts as a North Star for all other identities, is not meant to be divvied up. You cannot invest your ultimate worth in two different sources. This collapses into bankruptcy. You cannot be loyal to two masters. This leads to treason. You cannot listen to two inner voices. This becomes a cacophony.

Amidst thousands of competing identities, the Christian faith also invites you to realize an identity that gives definition to your worth, loyalties, and true self. However, unlike those identities created by people who would want to control you, the identity that springs forth from the Christian faith is not pushed on you, but gifted to you.[15]

As we will see, this identity was purchased at great cost to the Giver, so that it might be both sufficient for standing

---

[14] If you know someone who has been chronically abused, you can see how their sense of who they are has eroded their belief that they are worthy of value and respect.

[15] Ephesians 2:8

against the weight of the world and forging inner confidence in the recipient.

Perseverance

Sooner or later, and probably much sooner, life is going to get hard – really hard. Dreams evaporate. Relationships implode. People die. Things fall apart.

There is no question of *whether* you will suffer in this life; the only question is *to what extent* you will suffer. When pain and struggles do come your way, where will you find the strength to keep going? How can you pick yourself up off the floor and continue on, and how can you help others to do the same?

The ability to persevere through adversity varies greatly from person to person. I have seen people admirably endure the kind of personal difficulty that would crush the average person. I have seen others whom seem to fall into crisis if the slightest challenge is thrown at them. What accounts for this wide spectrum in a person's capability for perseverance? To be sure, some people seem endowed with an innate stoicism that keeps them cool under pressure. But what if you're not one of those people? I, for one, am not. For those whom it is not inside of themselves to gracefully endure pain and suffering, we must find the strength to persevere from a place outside of ourselves.

Perhaps the greatest way to handle the adversity of the present, to face suffering head on, is confidence in the future. This confidence must go beyond mere optimism, the ever-fickle feeling that things might magically turn out in a way acceptable to our preferences. Our confidence must be in a well-founded hope. The Christian faith claims to offer just this kind of hope, which allows even average people to persevere on days when they would rather give up.[16]

Perseverance, even in the face of great suffering, is possible for us because Christians worship a God who persevered through suffering for the hope of a beautiful future for both us and Godself.[17]

Ethics

If you were to ask the average person, irreligious or religious, to describe the primary purpose of religion, they likely would tell you it is to instill a sense of morals and values.

The idea of religion as the magnetizing power behind an ethical compass is as ancient as religion itself. It begins with acknowledging that personal *morality* without communal formation tends to be self-seeking. *Ethics*, in contrast, is a system of right and wrong that claims some objective authority to form that individual's morality.

How do you get people in our society to do fewer bad things and do more good things? Religion can be harnessed as a system of ethics to tell others your conception of what is good and what is bad, while incentivizing good behavior and threatening some form of punishment for bad behavior. This reason for religious involvement is often so compelling that I've known people who personally don't genuinely believe in religion themselves, but still attend church. Why? They find it useful for making their children better behaved.

Of course, any religion can provide an ethical framework for conducting our lives. The Christian faith is no different. However, ethical living – while certainly flowing from the claims of Christianity – is not Christianity. You don't

---

[16] 2 Peter 1:5-7; James 1:12
[17] Hebrews 12:2

need to believe in God to behave ethically. There is no shortage of examples of irreligious people with admirable morals and religious people acting as if they had none.

There are secular philosophies that are just as ethically demanding as any religion. Many otherwise irreligious people have very strong views about what is right and wrong, just and unjust. We simply don't need religious belief in a deity to make a pragmatic moral code or relatively moral people. Yet whether people adhere to traditional world religions or secular philosophies, all of them have a tendency to fall to another sociological and psychological function of ethics. Subscribing to a system of ethics allows us to identify the "good" people and the "bad" people. By creating mental categories of good and bad people, we grant a pressure release valve for our anger at the bad people and a pipeline for associating ourselves with the good people. Essentially, religious and secular philosophies make their adherents exclusionary of others.

The Christian faith claims to be different by offering an ethical compass that doesn't just point us to moral behavior, but also cultivates a humble compassion for those who are navigating by other compasses. When it actually is practiced faithfully, it ruins our desire to separate others into categories of good and bad, but maintains our commitment to the good.[18] Essentially, it is inclusive of others.

If our Teacher, Jesus himself, died to save his self-proclaimed enemies, it should be difficult for a Christian to maintain such a harsh distinction towards anyone else.[19]

The One Door That Lets Us Outside

It should be evident that even if I like the idea of having real purpose, taking part in a grand story, finding my truest

---

[18] John 8:1-8; Romans. 2:1-3; James 4:11-12
[19] Luke 23:34; Romans 5:8; Titus 3:2-7

identity, gaining the power to persevere, and developing an inclusive set of ethics, merely *wanting* it all to exist doesn't make it so.

I can pretend I live and breathe for some worthwhile purpose that extends past my last breath, but for that purpose to genuinely exist it must have been established long before I ever took my first breath.

I can imagine that the drama of history is progressing forward, but to do that I need to know that this grand story provides an objective sense of progress and regress written by someone other than the victors.

I can manufacture self-esteem from within myself, but my true sense of identity and self can't be known until there is legitimate authority that tells me who I really am and what I'm really worth.

I can wish for the best in bad situations, but I can't know if everything is going to turn out truly alright in the end unless I know the ending.

I can boldly fight injustice in my community and in my nation, but I can't be a fully ethical instrument of reconciliation until I come to believe that my enemies may one day be my brothers and sisters.

Now, from any of these five statements, you may have noticed a mental protest within yourself. You may feel that you already possess some or all of these traits without subscribing to the Christian faith. Of course you can *feel* that you do. This is entirely normal. You can even *act* as if you do. This too is fairly common. Here then is the rub that most people spend their entire lives avoiding: without an *objective point of reference* beyond my own and everyone else's subjectivity, I will never have any logical grounds to know what is true about the most important questions humanity has wrestled with.

Any beliefs I might have about truth, purpose, ethics, or justice – can always be neutralized by an ever-so-simple rebuttal of, *"Says who?"* My subjective experience of the world will merely bounce off others' subjective experiences, each of us fabricating just enough meaning for our lives to stave off the leviathan of despair lurking beneath the surface of our psyches. We will all be playing a well-meaning but delusional game of make-believe. Then we will die.

Cheery proposition, right? Yet there is good news to the existential conundrum of human existence. The Christian faith believes that an objective point of reference, an "Absolute Real" if you will, does exist. Not only does this objective point of reference exist, but that it has also revealed itself to us. This second belief is of equal importance. It means we are not groping around in the empirical or philosophical dark hoping to find the objective point of reference. The Absolute Real is not hiding from us. There is good news that life can be much more beautiful, but remember, we can't wish such good news into existence. This revolutionary way of living can't be imagined. It can only be revealed. It must come to us as revelation beyond human consensus or popular vote.

Remember, Pascal's Wager is not whether we should believe Christianity simply on the chance that these revolutionary beliefs might be true. The wager is that if we wish these revelations could be true, then it would be a poor gamble to not give thoughtful consideration to the very source that could authenticate it all. In other words, if you spent even a few months considering the claims of the Christian faith and found them unconvincing, the cost to you has been very little. [20] However, if you declined to seriously consider the answers to the most pressing problems of human existence and those answers are indeed true, the cost to you, others, and perhaps even the world itself could not even begin to be tallied. With our ample modern distractions, most irreligious and even

---

[20] Psalm 25:5; John 8:32

religious people simply don't realize what is at stake – our very reason for living – before a thoughtful investigation is made.

If we don't want to miss out on what might be capable of changing not only our own lives, but the lives of those we love, this is a wager worth making. Like *Alice in Wonderland*, many people spend their lives walking through proverbial door after door in the hope of it leading to the fulfillment of their deepest needs. Yet we open one door just to stare straight into another. We open the next door only to step into another locked room for which we have no key.

Could it be though that our purpose, story, identity, perseverance, and ethics may be just behind an unlocked door we've never opened? Perhaps it is a door we have never even noticed? We may even find that this door does not lead us into some other room – just another constraining ideological dogma under a different name – but this door is the one door that lets us out in the open air to experience true freedom.

You might think a door of this importance would require us to fashion a key of our own making to unlock it. It doesn't. Nothing is required of us. Everything has already been done for you.

We just need the revelation that will let us *see* the door. I will offer that this revelation will be both biblical and beautiful, that is, both timeless and transcendent. This, I believe, is the heart of the Christian faith.

FAITH HOPE LOVE

CHAPTER TWO
The Measure

It makes for good kitschy decor.

"Faith, hope, love" appears on decorative plaques on the walls of homes that are otherwise non-religious. Wedding vows too. If you're struggling to include a Scripture verse in your matrimonial ceremony, First Corinthians 13:13 is a safe, sentimental pick. After all, who can argue with the Bible's famous, "And now these three remain: faith, hope, and love. But the greatest of these is love"? As a matter of principle, I never let a bride and groom choose this passage.

It's a brilliant truth that has been reduced to an almost meaningless cliché. A pseudo-spiritual phrase that serves as a placeholder for our own projections of whatever we want it to mean.

Yet I offer that this is the very passage we should frame the heart of Christianity with. Faith, hope, and love was not originally a cliché. It is how the first Christians understood the message they were taking to the ends of the earth.

Let's first look at the wider context of our passage in First Corinthians:

> "Love never ends. As for prophecies, they will pass away; as for tongues, they will cease; as for knowledge, it will pass away. For we know in part and we prophesy in part, but when the perfect comes, the partial will pass away. When I was a child, I spoke like a child, I thought like a child, I reasoned like a child. When I became a man, I gave up childish ways. For now we see in a mirror dimly, but then face to face. Now I know in part; then I shall know fully, even as I have been fully known. So now faith, hope, and love abide, these three; but the greatest of these is love." (9-13, ESV)

This teaching comes from a man named Saul of Tarsus. Before Saul became a Christian and a leader of early Christianity, he actually led the first wave of persecution to arrest and kill Christians. [21] He was very religious, but his religiosity was devoid of love. However, on the way to round up more followers of Jesus, God appeared to Saul of Tarsus and identified himself as Jesus. Shocked and suddenly self-aware of his own blindness, Saul's life would be irrevocably transformed by the love of God. [22] It even reflected a change in identity. Taking on the name Paul, the Greek version of the Hebraic Saul, Paul moved past his previous ethnocentric religion for a new understanding of faith that would be accessible to all people without condition. Today, he is simply referred to by Christians as Saint Paul or the Apostle Paul.

Given this dramatic conversion from a spiteful Christian-hunter to a missionary and eventual martyr, it

---

[21] Acts 7:54-8:3
[22] Acts 9:1-19

makes sense that Paul places a special emphasis on explaining how important love is to the nature of the Christian faith. We cannot know God apart from love. Though Paul claims inspiration directly from God's Spirit, he's also humble enough to realize that he neither possesses the fullness of love nor the fullness of the knowledge of God.

Paul clarifies that we can only understand true love, only understand God, only understand our own self, as one "seeing in a mirror dimly." One day though, we shall see "face to face." This is certainly a bold hope to have.

Yet until that glorious day, Paul admits he can only "know in part." There is, again, shocking humility in this admission. The ambassador of Christianity to the Greek and Roman world realized he was proclaiming a message only as one describes the sun at the break of dawn. There is so much more to come. There is also a twist.

"But then I shall know fully," he says, "even as I have been fully known."

Spiritual knowledge, the kind of revolutionary knowledge at the heart of the Christian faith, is not merely a propositional, abstract truth. It is not an object to be studied as if in a laboratory. It is not so much something we intellectually believe as it is something we relationally experience. How can this be?

A Biblical Measure for Truth

It is easy for us to sentimentalize faith, hope, and especially love. Our culture decided that these words are "good" words. We have a funny habit – English speakers at least – of taking our favorite good words and denuding them of meaning. We sanitize them to make them safe for public consumption. This way, everyone can use faith, hope, and love without even being questioned for what they might mean by it.

Paul, however, pushes us in the opposite direction. Instead of stripping these words of meaning, he imbues them with significance. Instead of letting them be light, airy, and safe, he hangs so much weight on them that the world itself could be swept away – but faith, hope, and love would still remain.

Faith, hope, and love are somehow relational. Paul expects one day to see the fullness of faith, hope, and love "face to face" and know it as he has been known by it. He expects to know faith, hope, and love as one would know an intimate friend. How could he though? Aren't these words just concepts strung together for poetic embellishment? Not for Saint Paul. Not for the Christian.

Faith, hope, and love are words that have been made relational by God. By virtue of the Creator's presence in human history, the heart of Christianity has become inseparably defined by these three words. To know faith, hope, and love to the fullest is to know God. To know God is to know the fullest of faith, hope, and love. Why is this important? Because it gives you some objective measure to evaluate my understanding of the essential nature of the Christian faith.

It is not enough to simply say, "These conservative Christians have it wrong with this, and those progressive Christians have it wrong with that." If so, what I offer would be only my personal and biased opinions. To be sure, I am still applying *my interpretation* of the Bible and the historic Christian faith. Despite many people's claim to "just follow the Bible," no one actually does. It's not that they're not trying to, but rather because no person can come from a place of pure objectivity. Everything must be interpreted.

What I am attempting here is to provide some external justification for the heart of Christianity outside of myself, particularly in a source that establishes a level of objectivity that can only exist if God is involved in God's own creation. *If* the Christian faith is true, *then* it stands to reason that the Bible is a more objective and reliable guide about spiritual reality than my personal opinions.

Quite unlike what you may have heard about the Bible coming together like a children's game of telephone, full of increasingly comical mistakes with every new copy made, the Bible was not put together in this way. Its diverse composite books, written over a period of approximately 1100 years[23] and often distributed across two or three continents, preserved the original texts with unparalleled precision for any book in the ancient world.[24] What kind of precision? Of all the textual variants or copyist discrepancies that exist in the 25,000 pieces of biblical manuscripts, less than one percent might change the meaning of the text and zero affect any essential Christian belief.[25]

The books that make up what Christians call the New Testament were written entirely during the first century and within the lifetimes of either first- or second-generation followers of Jesus. When Christianity became legal in the fourth century, Christian leaders publicly convened to confirm the contents of their Holy Scriptures in a process called *canonization*. This was achieved by a relatively simple and uncontroversial consensus. How? All but four books of today's Bible already were being treated as a de facto Bible by the beginning of the third century.[26] Through 300 years of persecution, the Bible was organically curated by multiple

---

[23] If one includes oral tradition, the Bible may have come together over a period of up to 1400 years (1300 BCE - 100 CE) or more.

[24] What Christians call the "Old Testament" did undergo multiple revisions early in its development and today we are generally aware of how that development happened. In some sense, it is better to understand parts of the Old Testament as a "holy conversation" rather than a holy monologue.

[25] Craig L. Blomberg, Can We Still Believe The Bible? An Evangelical Engagement With Contemporary Questions (Grand Rapids, MI: Brazos Press, 2014), 25.

[26] Origen (a Christian scholar) of Alexandria's 3rd century did not include Jude, 2nd Peter, and the 2nd and 3rd Epistles of John.

cultures and languages, and free from any imperial or excessively institutional interference in its confirmation process.

As a practical note, that means when you see different translations or versions of the Bible today, you're not seeing different competing versions of the Bible as if the Bible has been changed over time. You're seeing different English translations of the original Greek or Hebrew languages from the same uncontested Bible. A person may or may not believe the messages or stories contained within the pages of the Bible, but it is certainly a reliable witness to the beliefs of its original authors.

This reliable witness, a guide which Christians have historically described as *authoritative*, tells us that any healthy understanding of Christianity must deeply reflect a narrative of faith, hope, and love that is mirrored by the relational revelation of God. If a proposed interpretation of Christianity has no room for faith that God has been at work in the human story, or leads us to despairing for the future, or makes us hateful toward any neighbor, then this interpretation must be rejected.

This is not a matter of picking and choosing verses in the Bible. At best, that is intellectually lazy. At worst, we make a Christianity of our personal preferences. No, faithful interpretation is much harder for Christians. We are meant to wrestle with every verse until we can submit to an interpretation that is congruent with the principles of faith, hope, and love.

The Bible serves as both our conversation partner and our teacher in trying to ascertain the heart of the Christian faith. It creates a timeless revelation capable of breaking through our limited time-bound perspective.

A Measure for Everyone Else

But what if the Bible isn't that guide for you? What if the idea of relational revelation seems hard to accept? What if you believe some of the stories contained within it, but find it closer to Aesop's Fables[27] than a witness of encounters with the God of the universe? If that's the case, I would like to offer one other measure of objectivity.

Utility as a reliable measure of truth, as mentioned earlier, reduces truth to an individualized, subjective tool for purposes of personal consumption. Like the sentimentalizing of faith, hope, and love, utility robs truth of its very meaning. Truth judged only by its utility ceases to be truth. Like skillful flattery or a politician's campaign promises, something can be entirely useful and entirely a lie.

Yet there is a measure I think the non-religious can use with some degree of confidence.

"Beauty is truth, truth beauty."

The English Romantic poet, John Keats, penned this simple line in 1819. Keats was alluding to the belief that beauty could speak to a reality greater than an object or idea could on its own. Beauty may even be capable of showing us what is really true, and exposing what is false.

Not surprisingly, such a grand adage is disputed by many. Today, we have a difficult enough time agreeing what beauty is, much less distinguishing between truth and lies. Yet, if Keats' maxim can't be considered on par with the laws of physics, it certainly makes friends with this scientific field. Mathematician Ian Stewart wrote, "In physics, beauty does not ensure truth, but it helps. In mathematics, beauty must be true

---

[27] Ancient Greek folktales used for the education of children.

— because anything false is ugly."[28]

The beauty we're referencing is not physical beauty. A Hebrew prophet named Isaiah (who predicted the coming of Christ 700 years in advance) said, "He had no form or majesty that we should look at him, and no beauty that we should desire him." [29] There is nothing inherently true about a physically attractive person or an aesthetically pleasing painting. "Elegance" might steer us in a more accurate direction. The beauty Keats and Stewart are getting at is the kind of graceful and transcendental interaction between the subject and the object, the viewer and the viewed.

How does this work? Whether it's a mathematical formula, a scientific theory, a moving poem, or a fantastic film, a small voice in the hidden reaches of our subconscious, awoken by truth, speaks up. Our soul, or whatever you might call it, is stirred. For just a moment it whispers to our conscience, "This! This is so right. This is beautiful." In the most extreme cases this has been labeled as Stendhal syndrome, where people in awe of great works of art have experienced dizziness, fainting, and even heart attacks.[30]

Conversely, ugliness hits us as well. Ugliness is unnecessarily complicated and disjointed, crude and grotesque. Maybe you've seen a film made poorly enough to elicit these feelings, but all too often we sense it watching the news, watching ideologues give absurd partisan rants in between clips of the latest terrorist attack. Again, whatever our conscious rejection of the evil playing out before our eyes, that small voice from our subconscious again provides a nauseating feeling. Though we know not from where it comes, we hear internally, "This is not the way it was meant to be. This is ugly."

[28] Ian Stewart, *Why Beauty Is Truth: A History of Symmetry* (New York: Basic Books, 2008), 280.

[29] Isaiah 53:2

[30] Alexandra Thompson, "Beauty of the Botticelli 'Brings on Heart Attack'," *Daily Mail*, December 18, 2018.

None of this is spiritual. Or perhaps it all is. Either way, beauty seems to affect us far more than mere aesthetics. It provides a lens to help us see, an aid to help us hear, and a scale to help us weigh. Why though should we cordon off beauty as the signpost of truth to merely physicists and poets?

If both diverse spheres of the sciences and humanities have consistently observed that ugliness is falsity and beauty indicates truth – and this is good enough for such an unyieldingly objective discipline as mathematics – why shouldn't we apply this to faith and spirituality? This is not to say we should only look for beauty. One-dimensional criteria are historically dangerous, be it religious movements or scientific theories. Yet if whatever divine force behind the curtain of the universe made both truth and beauty, why shouldn't we expect to find the two dancing together across the plane of existence?

So it is not that I hope you will find the heart of the Christian faith intellectually overwhelming or so forceful in its reasoning you will be compelled to submit to it without a doubt in your mind. As I said, I've never seen anyone argued into the Kingdom of God. Rather, my hope is that you find the essential narrative of Christianity beautiful. That if you find yourself at some point *wishing* it was true, then by the principles of physics and mathematics it very well just might *actually* be true. In the very least we might agree that "beauty does not ensure truth, but it helps." Beauty points us to the transcendent in a way that mere arguments – even logically reasoned – cannot.

The heart of the Christian faith then should be a beautiful heart, even to someone who doesn't consider themselves attracted to religion. The heart of the Christian faith should also be a biblical heart, framed with the relationally connected meanings imbued in faith, hope, and love. We should expect to find both of these features together.

Bound Up In Love

One more thought on love though. Love, as perhaps one of the most privileged words in the English lexicon, is often used as a trump card to exonerate any behavior or negate any competing claim in our culture.

The twentieth century theologian C.S. Lewis crafted a thought experiment about the nature of Heaven and hell. In his book, *The Great Divorce*, a woman refuses to enter Heaven even after her own death. In what is regarded by many as the most poignant and painful chapter of the book, she demands that until God can guarantee her that she'll see her son in Heaven, she will protest in hell.

> *"I don't believe in a God who keeps mother and son apart. I believe in a God of Love. No one has a right to come between me and my son. Not even God. I hate your religion and I hate and despise your God. I believe in a God of Love."*

Even as we talk about faith, hope, and love, it may be tempting to elevate love over faith and hope. If God is real and relational, then God is certainly more than one-dimensional in God's attributes, but those other attributes may make us uncomfortable. When I begin to wrestle with the heart of Christianity, I might be tempted to say to myself, "Well, whatever this God of faith demands of me, I don't need to comply because all I need is love. Whatever this God of hope requires of me, I don't need to respond because all I need is love."

If God is love, and I believe God is, we should be cautious about using the concept of love as a weapon to keep God at a distance or to mitigate the importance of our personal response. The more we pursue one, the closer we should find ourselves coming to the other.

The Bible says the greatest virtue is love, but love is not a truth designed to knock down other truths. It is the greatest truth because it is the infinite truth. One day, when we are face to face with our Maker, we will no longer need faith or hope. God, Love Itself, will be before us. There will be no doubt left in anyone's mind. Until that day comes, all truths – if they are genuine truths – are held together. Love is the glue that binds them. Love is the song they all sing. Faith, hope, and love can never be set against one another, but are bound up together in sublime union.

Now that we've established the wager and measures, the structure of this book is framed with this understanding of 1 Corinthians 13:13 in mind. The heart of Christianity is faith, hope, and love, and it is love that permeates the story. I confess I hesitated to stick to this telling of things. In some ways, love doesn't simplify the explanation of the Christian faith, but complicates it. However, I could not escape the conclusion that to start or end any other way may not necessarily be incorrect, but it would be too mechanical. Like attending a wedding where you know neither the bride or groom, a Christianity of "just-the-facts" feels awkwardly detached. For all its complexity, this story begins in love and is completed in love, and I believe it is more than worth whatever additional effort it takes to understand the story on such personal terms.

Accordingly, the first explanation of Christianity begins with God's *love for creation*. The next section then explains the *faith in the past* of Christianity. Then again, we return to love, but this time God's *love from Heaven*. The following segment deals with the nature of the Christian's *hope in the future*. Finally, we turn back to how God's *love for the world* is concretely established in our own lives. The book then concludes with an exploration of what it looks like to respond to this story and the most common hesitations people have about embracing it.

This is, of course, not the only way to explain the Christian faith. Catholic and Eastern Orthodox traditions would certainly explain it a little differently, though I have tried to be implicitly inclusive of their contributions to historic Christianity. While I am now a Presbyterian minister of a relatively diverse church plant, at different times in my life I have been a Protestant of many flavors and even an agnostic. These spiritual journeys have inescapably influenced the understanding of my own faith and how I present it to others.

This is also not a claim of offering a formulaic recipe that condemns those who may lack the theological breadth or depth afforded by years of study. The Christian message, one sufficient in bringing those who trust it into relationship with God, has been proclaimed before in a space that wouldn't fill a single page.[31] The "essentials of Christianity" refers to those beliefs that set down the foundation for spiritual flourishing in the Christian, and missing any of them, a Christian would suffer significant spiritual hindrance. Said another way, my goal is not to be the arbiter of who is a "true" Christian, but rather to identify those markers of a holistic and healthy Christian faith.

These caveats disclosed, I have set out to make an explanation of the Christian faith that is clear, brief, and linear – each part of the narrative flowing from and building on the one before it. It is biblically rooted and I hope it offers nothing new to Christianity, but rather Christianity offered to the reader in a new way.

May you find the heart of Christianity as surprising as you find it beautiful.

---

[31] Acts 2:14-39; Acts 17:16-34; even Galatians 1:4

CHAPTER TWO The Measure

CHAPTER THREE
Love Through Creation

The end can only make sense in light of the beginning. This is where our story starts. This is where all stories start.

In the beginning, our Hebrew sages[32] tell us, there was a deep void. A sprawling darkness. Chaos. As best we can wrap our minds around it, there was nothing.

In the beginning, our scientists tell us, there was no space-time. No light. No laws of physics. Not even empty space. As best we can wrap our minds around it, there was nothing.

Then, *something* happened.

Our Hebrew sages tell us that God spoke into the nothingness, "Let there be light." The Christian faith still uses Latin to describe this event, *creatio ex nihilo*. God performed

---

[32] Likely ancient Hebrew priests.

"creation out of nothing." Suddenly, there was order and energy. The light was separated from the darkness.[33]

Our scientists tell us that the nothingness burst into an unimaginably brilliant light. Suddenly, there were laws of physics. Energy was separated into matter and non-matter.

The story goes on. Most scientists say the universe has existed 13.8 billion years, but since time itself is contingent on matter and gravity, measuring time is also relative to your position in the universe. The Hebrew sages register similar ambiguity. The first "day" of creation is called *yom*, which can also mean an undetermined era of time.

Billions of years of light and matter exploded outward into the nothingness. Even what we typically perceived as "empty" space pressed into absolute nothing. The laws of physics, seemingly perfectly tuned by "random" cosmological constants, allowed the universe to keep existing. Yet it did not merely exist as a static universe. It vibrated with the action of galaxies, solar systems, stars, planets. If anyone had been witness to the cosmic fireworks show, it would have been considered quite the display. Yet life, at least on earth, has only existed for a blink of the cosmic eye.

Scientists say life started with very simple forms. The Hebrew sages who compiled the first creation story[34] found in Genesis 1 agree with our scientists, that life moved from the most simple of observable creation, plants, and eventually worked its way up to the most complex, mammals. No scientist is sure how or when life started, but they theorized that it began in some perfectly positioned primordial dirt. The Hebrew sages acknowledge even humanity comes from this modest

---

[33] Genesis 1:1-5
[34] There were two origin accounts compiled in Genesis by Hebrew scholars based on the prevailing cosmologies of the time. Since their goal was teaching theology and not science, they were not bothered by their divergent chronologies and details.

origin. From the dust we came, the biblical author of Job writes, and to dust we will return.[35]

In a poetic sense, it seems only fitting that life would come along, that something would become capable of appreciating the universe it was a part of. Yet in raw probabilities, it should have never happened.

Francis Crick, the brilliant multidisciplinary scientist who sought to discredit any belief in God, confessed in his book *Life Itself*, "The origin of life appears at the moment to be almost a miracle, so many are the conditions which would have had to have been satisfied to get it going." However, this statement is not to imply support from some kind of "God-of-the-gaps" faith, where our belief in a deity temporarily fills in the missing spaces of our scientific knowledge and retreats when a more rational explanation emerges. A Christian faith like this suppresses our curiosity and eventually retreats into irrelevance and obscurity. I am more interested in the sense of wonder behind Crick's acknowledgment than trying to poke holes in any Darwinian evolutionary theory. The human experience of wonder is itself far worthier of contemplation.

The line between the *almost* miraculous and the *actually* miraculous might be fuzzier than we realize. Granted, when Crick found the universe almost miraculous, he meant he deemed it inexplicable. I too find the universe almost miraculous, but much in the same way I marvel at Beethoven's Fifth Symphony. I want to understand the composition of instruments and notes, but I also want to understand the composer.

Why is There Something Instead of Nothing?

Scientists and biblical storytellers are hardly in as much conflict as the materialist atheist and the literalist Christian

---

[35] Job 34:14-15

want us to imagine. If anything, their accounts are surprisingly similar regarding the universe's origins. Their major divergence is in their central purpose. Science tells us the *how*, but rarely the *why*. Religion occasionally makes claim to the *how*, but primarily exists to tell us the *why*.

Religion, at least any religion that seeks to be in tune with reality and not label existence an illusion, must grapple with the *how* as it is best understood so that it can provide the most plausible *why*. So why is there some-thing instead of no-thing? Why many things instead of one thing? Why is there this wondrous, terrifying, beautiful universe at all, much less with sentient beings able to experience it?

The Christian faith does provide an answer to these questions, and that answer is found in the nature of God. A disciple of Jesus named John, who was part of Jesus' innermost circle of disciples, famously said that "God is love." [36] Yet remember, this love is far more robust than the limited connotations of our modern vocabulary. In the Bible, love always corresponds with actions, and those actions are always harmonious with God's character.

The Christian faith says that the universe – particularly one with diversity, beauty, and life – flows from the love of God. Though our dynamic cosmos inspires wonder in the believer and skeptic alike, the formation of life is not *actually* miraculous. Life is *almost* miraculous. Why do I agree with Crick? Miraculous implies the impossible. Miraculous is what should almost certainly never be, but is. For the Christian faith, the creation of the cosmos and all life within it cannot be described in this way, because creation itself is a logical implication of God's character. Creation is a symphonic expression of God's love.

---

[36] 1 John 4:8

The Triune God

You might wonder though, how is making our universe an act of love? How is formation of sentient life an implication of God's character? Couldn't God just have been lonely? Ironically, or perhaps fittingly again, the only rational answer to this question is found in the most irrational of Christian beliefs. Christians, formally since the fourth century, and informally since the second century, have understood God as possessing three distinct personalities [37] who coexist in perfect unity.

The *Early Church* – the era of Christianity before Constantine legalized it in 313 CE – did not casually formulate this mysterious idea. The concept of a Triune God only emerged as Christians tried to make sense of seeing one God in three major ways. The God they read about in Hebrew Scriptures, the God they recognized as Jesus of Nazareth in human form, and the God they saw blowing about like wind in the Early Church. Though neither word is found in the Bible, Christians call this understanding of God the Trinity, or Triune God.

In one sense, while it is not meant to be accepted on faith as a contradiction, the Trinity is, by definition, a mystery. It has often been said tongue-in-cheek by Christians that if you think you completely understand the Trinity, you probably are committing a heresy (that is, an incorrect view of God). Imagine if someone who had only ever seen two-dimensional objects was asked to comprehend a three-dimensional object, something incorporating both the attributes of a two-dimensional object, and also something more at the same time. With such a finite experience informing that person, the concept of a three-dimensional object would feel perhaps

---

[37] The classical language is actually three "divine persons," but as long as you don't interpret "personalities" to mean divine schizophrenia, I believe this description is closer to what Christians are referring to in describing the Trinity.

impossible to conceptualize. Likewise, finite beings that we are, we cannot fully comprehend an entity that is both separate *and* one at the same time.

Still, Christians throughout history have tried to offer metaphors to help us understand, even if most of these metaphors are inadequate. Allow me to offer two though, one modern and more functional and one ancient and more relational.

Water as Creator, Redeemer, & Sustainer

A modern metaphor is H_2O, or water in its three states. Imagine before you three containers of water. One frozen solid, one liquid, and one evaporated gas.[38] Their chemical essence is the same, H_2O, and lined up next to one another they exist simultaneously in three distinct states. We can say the Trinity is like water in three states because even though the Triune God manifests Godself in three distinct personalities simultaneously, they all share the same essence of one God.[39]

This metaphor also hints at the central roles of each part of the Trinity. Though no role is exclusively performed by a single personality in the Trinity, they are known by their distinctive work. We can understand these three roles as God the Creator, God the Redeemer, and God the Sustainer.

The Creator is the *transcendent* personality of God, ruling outside of time and space. The Creator lovingly holds the universe in the Creator's hands. The Redeemer (aka Jesus Christ) is the *incarnational* personality of God, who joined humanity to save humanity. The Redeemer rescues us to bring

---

[38] For additional theological precision in our metaphor since the Triune God is unique, you can also imagine that these three containers of H_2O, are the only containers of H_2O in the universe.

[39] With H_2O, scientists have also identified a 'triple point', where the three states exist simultaneously within a single container. This may even be a better metaphor, but also runs close to the heresy of modalism, which incorrectly posited that one God changed into each of the three states.

us back to the Creator. The Sustainer (aka the Holy Spirit) is the *immanent* personality of God, working within time and space. While Christians tend to default to crediting the Creator or Redeemer for answered prayer or spiritual experiences, this is actually most often the work of the Sustainer subtly supporting, speaking to, and transforming those who seek to worship the Creator and the Redeemer.

The Creator, Redeemer, and Sustainer are all distinct personalities and they all share the same essence of one God.

A Dance as Father, Son, & Holy Spirit

Still, to understand the Triune God solely in terms of Creator, Redeemer, and Sustainer is limiting. The Trinity, while possessing distinct functions, is not purely functional. This is where an ancient metaphor can help us comprehend.

The metaphor comes from the Greek word, *perichoresis*, or circle dance. Imagine the Triune God as three dancers in such exquisite coordination it is as if they are of one mind. No dancer is more important than another. Every dancer is critical. All dancers are intimately connected. The fluidity of their movements blurs into something bigger than the dancers themselves – the dance. We can say the Trinity is like a divine dance, moving around in a beautiful harmony held together by loving communion.

This metaphor is important to our understanding God's character, and subsequently the reason for the universe, because the Trinity exists in perfect relational and communal love. You may have heard the Trinity described before as the Father, Son, and Holy Spirit, which we have just referred to as the Creator, Redeemer, and Sustainer respectively.[40]

Language like this is uncomfortable to some, because despite the Holy Spirit possessing classically feminine

---

[40] 2 Corinthians 13:14

associations in the Greek language, the exclusively masculine imagery of the Father and the Son can be viewed as perpetuating patriarchal sexism. However, the language of Father, Son, and Holy Spirit is not meant to be a statement against gender equality, but rather affirm the deeply relational nature of the Triune God. God is love and central to the very essence of God is relationship. This relationship between parent and child is one of the most powerful relational pairings within humanity, and would have acutely resonated with Jesus' audience.

Since God is not an actual male, gendered discussions about God should be handled thoughtfully, but God's gendered expressions are essentially a prelude to God's relational attributes. To talk about God's character without talking about a relational dynamic would be to miss the heart of who God is. The Triune God is indispensably relational.

The Surprising Importance of the Trinity

Yet is the Trinity *really* an essential belief to Christianity? After all, if the Trinity was not formally codified as Church doctrine until the 4th century, certainly there were people in the Early Church who did not have a clear concept of the Triune God. Perhaps more important to our exploration of the heart of the Christian faith, am I saying that if you don't fully understand the Trinity, you can't be considered a genuine Christian?

To be clear, a perfect understanding of the Trinity cannot be required as part of a Christian's essential beliefs, if for no other reason than the Trinity is a mystery. Just as no one can perfectly understand the ten-dimensional [41] nature of string theory, no one can perfectly understand the omni-dimensional nature of the Trinity. However, I offer that we do

---

[41] At least ten dimensions. By some estimates, it could be more.

need to believe in the basic assumptions of the Trinity, that God is somehow intrinsically in perfect relationship and community with Godself. This places the Trinitarian paradox on God's infinite nature and not on our finite comprehension.

Why are these beliefs so crucial to accept? Without the basic assumptions of community within the Trinity, God cannot be love. Whatever is intrinsic to the nature of God had to exist before the first light burst from the nothingness eons and *yoms*[42] ago. A God that only eventually *became* loving could not truly be God. Whatever God is, God has always been, but let us take this to a more profound claim.

We established that one of Jesus' closest disciples, Saint John, says God does not merely extend love as you or I might, but that God *is* love. How could Saint John say something so magnificent as to declare that God is love and not simply loving? Saint John, even without a formal understanding of the Trinity, understood from his unique experience of living alongside Jesus what this kind of love entails. Love requires more than one person. A community requires more than two persons.

If God was radically singular, God would have no way to give or receive love, and there would be no harmonious community. Only a God that has always existed as three-in-one and one-in-three is capable of being characterized as both perfect love and perfect community. God is love because God has always given love back and forth between Father, Son, and Holy Spirit from before time began.

This is why an appreciation of the nature of the Triune God, as imperfect as our understanding may be, is at the heart of the Christian faith. It allows us to be more than merely optimistic that God is loving, but trust that love is at the very center of God's character.

---

[42] That is Hebrew for "a really, really long period of time."

Still, there is one more reason why the Triune nature of God is important, and it answers why there is some-thing instead of no-thing. If God is a perfect community of love, then we should not be surprised at the universe's existence. It may be an inexplicable event to materialist atheism, but the Christian faith does not even consider it a miracle.

After all, a radically singular god may or may not have desired to create anything – perhaps if a solitary god was bored, but one still doesn't necessitate the other. The Triune God, however, has always been a community of love, and love always creates. Love creates joy and peace. Love creates intimacy and self-giving. Love creates relationship and community. If this is true about love, how could God be love and *not* create?

God's love is not an inward-focused infatuation, but an ever-inviting passion. Even before creation, God's love was perpetually shared among the Trinity, bursting at its divine seams. Like an inspired artist, it is inevitably a creative love freely expressed, and so we see God's *love through creation*. It artfully expands outward in all directions. In the Big Bang, it literally expanded space-time itself. The entire universe, condensed to something smaller than a pinhead, gloriously erupted in creative love. The cosmos itself is an expression of this overflow of love generated by the Trinity.

The love of the Triune God kept creating and creating, until from out of the microbes of the dust, the first humans arose.

Made in the Image of the Triune God

Some people have said God was lonely, so he created people to love. However, this notion brings us back to a deficient God, one that neither had the character of love from the beginning nor creates out of love. The Christian faith affirms that we were not only made *in* love, but made *for* love.

In the Hebrew creation stories of Genesis, God says, "Let us make humanity in our image."[43] That is, let us make humanity capable of reflecting the love and community that always existed within the Triune God.

Being made in what the Christian faith calls the *imago Dei* also means something profound about our value. Other ancient cultures had their own creation stories. For example, in the Mesopotamian narrative of *Enuma Elish*, humanity is made as servants to the gods. In the related Gilgamesh epic, it's clear that the gods keep eternal life to themselves and consign humanity to perpetual death. The Hebrews would have certainly been familiar with some of these stories, so it's remarkable that they choose not to tell entirely new creation narratives, but to incorporate the origin myths of their pagan neighbors.

It was as if the Hebrew sages were saying to their whole known world, "You have said the gods are capricious and abusive, but we have good news! They are not. The good news is that there is one God above all other gods, and this God is gracious and merciful. Let us retell the origin story."

When God placed God's image in humanity, it was a stamp of intrinsic worth and value for all people. Not just the wealthy or the rulers. Not just for men or a single ethnicity. All people, without exception, were created with equal worth and value. We were not created to be slaves or chess pieces in the divine intrigues of deities.

The stamp of the *imago Dei* in each person provides the objective grounding to believe that all people, without exception, were created in love and made for love.

---

[43] Genesis 1:26-27

So What? Trusting that I Am Not God

Being made in the image of God dignifies humanity in a way that even humanity itself struggles to recognize and honor, and yet being made in the image of God also says something else profound about humans – that we are not God. You may not find this to be a groundbreaking revelation, but our collective and individual failure to acknowledge this has led to untold heartbreak and suffering.

God's invitation to us is to trust God in all things, and this begins with us understanding that in addition to God's fundamental character of love, God is *sovereign*. Wrapped up in this grand word, sovereign, are two *omni* words, that is, God is the greatest and fullest source of some trait. The Christian faith affirms that God is *omniscient*, meaning all-knowing, and *omnipotent*, meaning all-powerful. Theologians in Judaism and Christianity have debated how far to take these words, with more contemporary theologians positing that God might have voluntarily given up a portion of his knowing or power so as to enter into a more vulnerable relationship with us. Still, all of these views understand God as possessing incomparably more wisdom and power than humanity.

Yet, I forget this truth all too often. I delude myself into thinking that I am wiser than God. I pretend that I have greater control of a situation in my life than God. In effect, by not trusting that God is wiser and in more control than I am, I am claiming my own sovereignty. I am claiming to be God.

Individually, this has led me down all sorts of paths that may have seemed like a good idea at the time, but in the long run did damage to my life and wounded my spirit. Writ large on the world, this is the same insolence that has fueled brutal tyrants and greedy corporate executives, even many of our venerated and "larger-than-life" cultural icons of art and music.

We may find it odd that ancient kings and emperors were considered divine by their subjects, but this is simply the logical endpoint for humans who do not trust that God is omniscient and omnipotent. There will always be some person or ideology to claim the sovereignty of divinity, and there will always be some people willing to place their trust in them.

So what must I trust instead as an implication of God's creative love? It is that since God is the creator, I am not. Since God is sovereign, I am not. If God lovingly made me with all wisdom and power, I can instead trust that when I come to understand God's will for me, I should faithfully obey it. I am not God, and thank God for that!

A Beautiful Purpose

When we look at the biblical text that describes the Triune God making humanity in God's image, we find that the Hebrew word for "image" can also be translated "idol." Now, if we think about idolatry at all, we normally consider it a bad thing. After all, God is God and we are not. Yet if God did not want us to pretend to be God, what could have possibly been the reason for God creating humans like walking and talking idols? The answer to this apparent contradiction is found in our purpose.

Ancient people, despite all their forms of superstition, were not stupid. We often imagine that polytheistic and animist religions prayed to their carved statues of wood and stone, but this would be a gross simplification. These adherents did not pray *to* their idols, but *through* their idols. These carved idols were meant to direct their hearts and minds to unseen deities and spirits.

It was meant to be the same with us. Bearing the image of God, we were made by God so that by our words and actions, those around us would direct their worship not to us, but through us to the God whose image we bear. We were meant to live such awe-inspiring lives that people would be brought to their knees in worship of the One who created our lives.[44]

Now let us pair the purposeful meaning behind us being made in the image of God with God's love through creation. In the second Hebrew creation story found in Genesis 2, God creates Adam and Eve. They may or may not have been meant to be taken as literal figures, but they were certainly meant to be taken as representative of our human story.

In the Hebrew, *Adam* literally means "humanity," and is constructed from the Hebrew word for "red," likely implying the red soil from which humanity sprung. *Eve* means "source of life," formed as the glorious pinnacle of creation on earth. She is said to be taken not from Adam's foot, which would convey misogynistic inferiority, and not from Adam's heart or head, which would convey puritanical ideals of piety or prudence. Surprisingly, for a narrative that was eventually written down in an otherwise highly patriarchal ancient near-east culture, Eve is taken from Adam's side.[45] This radically conveys intimacy and equality.

Amidst the life-giving springs of a garden called *Eden*, God walked with Adam and Eve in the cool breezes of the evening, meaning they knew God as a dear friend. They in turn were made to love one another, and out of love, create more life to foster a human community that would point back to the love of God.

Do you see the pattern? Both creation stories in Genesis 1 and Genesis 2 reveal God's creative love was meant to even be repeated in God's creation. Just like God's creative love expanded outward into time and space, so God's people

---

[44] Genesis 22:18; Hebrews 12:4
[45] Genesis 2:20-23

were meant to do the same. We are told that Adam and Eve were not meant to stay comfortably where they were formed. They are instructed by God to boldly leave the security of the garden to "be fruitful, and multiply, and fill the earth, and subdue it."[46]

This is not, however, a militaristic or capitalist subjugation of the earth. This is a reflection of what God did at the cosmos' advent, subduing the darkness with light, and subduing the chaos with harmony. Humans are to control the earth, but not for themselves. This would be a usurpation of God's sovereignty, humans attempting to play God again. We were meant to tend to the planet and all its inhabitants as stewards of God's gracious will. We were meant to be co-creators with God.

This is what humanity from the very beginning was meant to do. And how were we meant to do it? By filling the earth as faithful image bearers, selfless idols pointing to God, and living lives of light and harmony in loving community.

Yet practically speaking, what could this look like? It's probably more mundane that you might imagine.

Fred Rogers came of age at the conclusion of the Second World War. In 1946, he went to Dartmouth College, and continued his education at Pittsburgh Theological Seminary. Rogers became an ordained minister, but was attracted to the emerging technology of television. Eventually, this soft-spoken Presbyterian would go on to create *Mister Rogers' Neighborhood*, film almost one thousand episodes, receive four Emmy awards, and profoundly touch the lives of millions of children.

Most people are surprised to learn of Rogers' theological credentials and the devout lifestyle he maintained over the course of his life. We've become so accustomed to

---

[46] Genesis 1:28

religious people wildly waving their faith flag in public, sometimes obnoxiously so, that we often assume a personal faith means an irrelevant faith sequestered for private spiritual comfort. Yet motivating Rogers' work for all those years was a profound sense that every person was an image bearer of God. His close friend Amy Hollingsworth said, "At the center of Fred's theology of loving your neighbor was this: Every person is created in the image of God, and for that reason alone, he or she is valued – 'appreciated,' he liked to say."[47]

This belief wasn't simply a motivation to be nice or friendly, though he of course was both. Rogers' very purpose was based on the divine interaction as image bearer and the God whose image he was bearing. In a commencement address at Marquette University, he shared, "I believe that appreciation is a holy thing, that when we look for what's best in the person we happen to be with at the moment, we're doing what God does; so in appreciating our neighbor, we're participating in something truly sacred."

Fred Rogers tapped into the same divine reality that Adam and Eve were invited into, creating in such a way that filled the earth with God's love by filling the airwaves.

The medium will often vary, but the mission remains unchanged. This was, and still is, our beautiful purpose.

---

[47] Amy Hollingsworth, The Simple Faith of Mister Rogers: Spiritual Insights From the World's Most Beloved Neighbor (Nashville, TN: Thomas Nelson, 2007), 78.

FAITH HOPE LOVE

CHAPTER FOUR
Faith In The Past (In Three Acts)

Act I: Betrayal

We were given by God a bold and beautiful purpose. Then we ruined everything.

The Hebrew creation stories tell us that at some point shortly after God placed his image in humanity and created intimate relationship with us, we destroyed the relationship. You might recall a story about an apple and a talking snake somehow doing us in. This, however, is the children's picture-book version of the story, and not even an accurate version at that.

The narrative found in Genesis tells us that humanity was given complete freedom to live out the purpose God had created for us in filling the earth with light and harmony in loving community. The one prohibition was a single tree in the garden. Our first parents were told not to eat from the fruit of that tree.[48]

Now it's often been argued accusingly that God seems to be the one tempting humanity with this tree. Isn't this some kind of divine entrapment? Yet to interpret the story in this hyper-literal way misses the point. The forbidden tree represents the necessary conditions for genuine trust and love to exist between God and humanity. Trust can only exist when there is choice to distrust. Love can only exist when there is a choice to be estranged. In a lush garden full of fruit-bearing plants and trees – including the certainly superior and aptly named Tree of Life – there was simply a mere tree that God declared off limits. God even explains why it is forbidden, to eat of this tree will lead to death.

The question this is meant to bring us to is not, "Why would God tempt humanity?" No ancient Hebrew sage would have concluded this was the point of the Genesis narrative. Instead, this was meant to make us ask, "Why would humanity choose not to trust God?" It seems near madness to do the very thing God says will bring you ruin, but this primordial tale also tells my own story all too well. I am not only a descendent of Adam of Eve, I am Adam and Eve. Why?

Our Response to Anxiety

There's a serpent in the Genesis story that acts as the rationalizing force behind humanity's decision to rebel against God. This serpent has also been historically understood by Christians to represent Satan, which translates from Hebrew to "The Adversary" or "The Accuser." The Bible surprisingly contains relatively little mention of Satan's motives or origins,

---

[48] Genesis 2:15-17

so it is unwise to speculate too strongly what exactly Satan is.[49] Whether one believes Satan is a former angelic being that revolted against God, a sentient symbol of corruption feeding off our own capacity for wickedness, or some personification of spiritual evil spread out across the universe, no conception is any less real or any less our enemy.

The combined biblical accounts do make it clear that the Adversary, this enemy of God and accuser of humanity, cannot overcome God. It is not a contest of equals. Anything that opposes the goodness of God will inevitably be defeated.[50] Yet, like a terrorist hell-bent on chaos and mass casualties, the Adversary wants to kill, steal from, and destroy that which is most precious to God, those made in the image of God. [51] So the Adversary begins this genocidal plot by convincing humanity to create their own wedge between them and their Creator.[52] The argument was simple, but persuasive.

"God has forbidden this singular tree," he whispers with a forked tongue, "not because he wants to protect humanity, but because God wants to limit humanity."

Anxiety is a universal human emotion. To exist is to experience anxiety.[53] Since we cannot know the future, our not knowing inevitably creates apprehension about what is to come. We wonder, we worry, how our lives and the lives of those we love will turn out. If the worry is not for tomorrow, our minds drift to years from now. Even in the best possible conditions, supported by money, power, and technology, our individual and collective futures always tremble beneath the fear of uncertainty.

---

[49] Most of what we have heard about Satan comes from art and fiction, both medieval and modern.

[50] Spoiler alert: The Bible records Satan suffering an irreversible defeat by Jesus and then later complete destruction by God.

[51] John 10:10

[52] Genesis 3:1-7

[53] While anxiety can be so frequent that it can become a disorder, most people simply try to avoid anxiety by endless distractions.

Surely Eve must have been curious about what power the tree's fruit possessed. God had mentioned it contained the knowledge of good and evil. Could this power possibly alleviate whatever fears about the future vexed her? The Serpent, to its credit, knew exactly where to strike.

"God is holding out on you. God is *lying* to you," warned the Adversary. "He knows that if you eat of this tree, you will not die. Instead, you will become like God yourself."

Like Adam, Eve, and every person who has ever lived, we cannot escape the presence of anxiety in our lives. It is not wrong to feel anxiety. Indeed, it is often a mark of self-awareness. Yet how we respond to anxiety matters immensely.[54] When our primordial parents were faced with this anxiety, humanity had two choices: Trust that God was sovereign over the future and that God had a good plan for us, or conclude God was lying the whole time. God would either be lying about his control and wasn't sovereign over the cosmos, or God would be lying about his goodness and didn't care about us. If either was true, then the Adversary was not actually our enemy, but our ally.

If God was lying, the Serpent offered the only other plausible solution to our anxiety. If God wasn't sovereign, then we were all on our own. I needed to take control. If God wasn't looking out for our good, then I needed to look out for my own self-interest. If there was a God at all, this God simply wasn't worth trusting. I could only trust myself. I needed to become, for all intents and purposes, my own God.

So "Humanity," or Adam, and descendants from the "Source of Life," or Eve, attempted to become their own gods by eating from the one tree that symbolized both genuine freedom and the potential for a destructive trajectory away from God. It was not the fault of a single man or woman. Both

---

[54] Philippians 4:6-7

partners ate the death fruit. It was a collective, communal decision to distrust God. Not only did it happen, but it is still happening. Every human being in every generation, both consciously and subconsciously, continues the same rebellion of our primordial parents. We were once in relationship, but now we have become estranged from God.

The Christian faith calls this estrangement, "The Fall."

The Fall as the Beginning of History

Much angst has been poured out about Darwinian evolutionary theory and the origins of humanity as some counter-narrative to the Christian story. As I said earlier, what happened before the arrival of the first humans made in the image of God and how literally the Genesis narrative is interpreted does not threaten the Christian faith. However, we should also be careful not to view the Fall story as purely mythological. It is meant to shine an introspective light on our own darkness. The same mistakes of the Fall are being repeated again and again today. We are no less culpable for the world's woes than Adam or Eve.

Furthermore, while the Fall's explanation of the human condition is perhaps the most crucial point to take from the Genesis story, it is still important to understand Genesis as inspired from historical realities. Christianity does, in contrast to almost all other religions, rest on its historicity. It is a faith that requires belief not just in particular morals or philosophies, but that there were real events in history that determined the course of history.

A Christian's *faith in the past* begins with seeing the Fall and the circumstances leading up to it, as the beginning of human history. Though Christians will differ on the circumstances and intensity of the Fall, this understanding of the origin of the human condition is widely agreed upon. At some point in the past God initiated a nurturing and life-giving relationship with a human community, and then that human community broke trust and relationship with God. We now live in the downstream of this history.

Why is this so important? It is because the rest of the Christian story seeks to rescue and redeem us from the negative effects of the Fall. Without some kind of Fall, there is no need for rescue. Without some kind of Fall, there is no need for a Redeemer. In fact, the Bible has said that God's mission ever since the Fall has been the reconciliation of the world to Godself. Reconciliation, however, means that we have first become estranged. If these concepts are to hold significant meaning, they must be connected to a corresponding moment in history that gives them meaning.

Defining Sin and the Effects of Estrangement

Anyone who has, at some point, tried to pray has felt the effects of estrangement from God. It feels as if our prayers are bouncing back from our bedroom ceilings or aimlessly cast away in the vast starry reaches of space. An intellectual assent to God's existence doesn't necessarily make us feel our prayers are getting through any more than I feel like my letter to my senator is being read. We may have to learn the hard way that most politicians don't listen to us, but we seem to intuitively know that there is some spiritual barrier, some metaphysical chasm, between the Creator and the creation.

The Christian faith pinpoints the source of this estrangement, almost synonymously so, with sin. As a word, "sin" is often incorrectly and cavalierly thrown around so much that few people, even religious people, know what it actually means. Sin is not making a technical mistake, like giving a wrong answer to a math problem or missing the wastebasket with some poorly aimed trash. Sin is not experiencing too much pleasure, as if grandma's desserts or a fine scotch posed an existential threat to our spiritual condition. Sin is not even breaking some religious rules, at least not in the form of dos-and-don'ts as we often presuppose religion is about.

What is sin then? Sin exists as a synchronous interplay between external actions and an internal condition. The act of sin is simply unjustifiable harm. It is damage that leads to disintegration. Yet the mentality that enables *individual* sins, particular acts of unjustifiable harm, can itself be traced back to a refusal to trust God's sovereignty and goodness while instead choosing to elevate myself in God's rightful place.

This should sound familiar. Without naming it, we have already discussed sin when people rejected God's omniscience and omnipotence, or when our primordial parents chose to assuage their anxiety by consuming that which they thought would give them god-like control. By foundationally being a distrust of God, sin as an internal condition disrupts and severs our relationship with God. Estranged from the source of truth, goodness, and beauty, even some of our best intentions begin to misfire or backfire with disastrous results.[55]

Becoming both a power unto itself as much as a choice made, the consequences of sin's estrangement echo outward like a stone cast into a glassy pool.

Brokenness in Relationships

The first observable consequence of sin, after we suffered a broken relationship with God, was to experience broken relationships within ourselves and with one another. In the Genesis narrative, we become aware of our nakedness and

---

[55] Associated with Greek tragedies, a frequent Greek word for "sin" in the New Testament is *harmartia,* which can be translated as "missing the mark."

pitifully try to cover things up.[56] This isn't a commentary on prudishness, but on the shame that our moral failures bring us. Our relationship with ourselves seems fundamentally marred and motivated by this shame. Before the Fall, we stood completely vulnerable and still felt completely accepted for who we were. Now, the list of our personal insecurities, some more rational than others, seems ever growing. From self-loathing to mental illness, we all suffer from some sort of brokenness in our sense of self.

Yet, if we can't cover up our fears of exposure and rejection, blaming others will have to do. When confronted by God, our primordial parents immediately begin a blame game. Adam blames God and Eve. Eve blames the Adversary. No one takes responsibility.

Behind every jealous act, gossip, rivalry, emotional manipulation, betrayal, and outright abuse, sin lurks in the background. We were made as inherently relational and social beings, but sin does what it always does. It kills, steals, and destroys what is good. Under the weight of sin, all human relationships – even our most cherished relationships – are under the constant threat of collapsing in on themselves.

Injustice to Our Neighbor

Sin didn't just ruin our relationships, as if only a reliable friend was harder to find now. Sin ushered in oppression and injustice against our neighbor. Some have criticized the Bible for its violence and cruelty. Rarely is such havoc approved of in any way by God; it is merely giving a painfully honest record of the human condition.

The Hebrew sages say our propensity to social and political wickedness is so great that by the sixth chapter of Genesis, they rewrote the Gilgamesh flood epic with a new

---

[56] Genesis 3:7

character named Noah as the world's last decent man. In the original Gilgamesh myth, it was a story of the gods plotting to destroy humanity out of capriciousness and perhaps jealousy. In the Hebrews' repurposed version, they reimagined such a calamity only as a tragic last resort of holding back evil in the world. For a people that suffered slavery under the Egyptian empire, they knew all too well that because of sin, economies and technology bend toward exploitation.

The Bible however, tells us that sin is behind more than just the explicit injustices, but also the idolatrous "isms" that more powerful or privileged factions of humanity have fought to justify. Though the Bible repudiates them all; racism[57], classism[58], nationalism[59], and heterosexism[60] have plagued us for thousands of years. In fact, the first "ism" recorded in Scripture is sexism. Because of the Fall, Adam and Eve descend from a life-giving relationship as complementary equals to a patriarchy where "[men] will rule over [women]."[61]

When our consciences became darkened by sin, we lost our ability to see our racially different, poor, immigrant, queer, or female neighbor as made equally in the image of God. In the fog of the Fall, our neighbors have either become objects of commodification or oppression.

Corruption to Our Earth

God originally made us to be stewards of God's planet, sentient beings capable of creating sustainable technology and elegant gardens. As long as we understood that the earth we lived on was God's possession and not our own, we would certainly be capable of building within an ecological balance.

---

[57] Romans 10:12; Acts 10:34-35
[58] 1 Corinthians 11:17-21; James 2:2-4
[59] Philippians 3:20; Hebrews 11:13-16
[60] Isaiah 56:4-5; Acts 8:26-40
[61] Genesis 3:16; Galatians 3:28

Yet the ripple effects from sin have done damage to even nature itself.

On one level, our mandate for harmonious dominion over the earth became distorted into a plot for self-centered domination. We sadly do not so much garden and tend the earth as we do harvest it for all it's worth. The ecological degradation and pillaging of the planet is an unfortunate byproduct of our sinful condition.

On another level, the Bible seems to say that the effects of sin have infected even nature itself. Perhaps beyond what we can say without speculating too much, creation seems to be groaning under a Fall-induced fever. [62] In response to the worsening effects of climate change, I have heard it said before by irreligious people that, "Mother nature is angry at us." Tsunamis, tornadoes, and hurricanes may very well have existed before the Fall, but the horrendous death and devastation they wreak upon humanity makes us feel as if something is not quite right. This should not be seen as a punishment by God, but rather like a detonated nuclear bomb, sin affects more than its immediate blast radius. It has become the radioactive fallout that has spread over the natural world.

The Christian faith confesses that because of our sin, God's earth is being corrupted. Our ecosystems are decaying at a rate, save for the mercy of God, that we seem unable or unwilling to recover from.

Death to Ourselves

Scripture declares that death is the last enemy of humanity.[63] Everything we love is ended by death: our friends, our family, and our own lives. Nothing can outlast death. Obviously, we as individuals will not. For that matter, nations,

---

[62] Romans 8:22
[63] 1 Corinthians 15:26

or cultures, or even solar systems will not outlast death. Time erodes all things. The universe itself, left to time, will die in what astrophysicists call a "heat death."

When humanity became estranged from God, death possessed humanity just as God had warned. However, it was not *just* physical death. In fact, Adam and Eve in the Genesis narrative still lived to ripe old ages that stretch our imagination. Neither is *all* physical death a tragedy. Sometimes, because of the irreversible declines in health many experience, death can feel like the only relief from suffering.

Death can even be part of the greater good. The cycle of life, death, and rebirth existed in nature as part of the creative process of the world before the existence of the first humans made in the image of God. In the last minute, three hundred million cells in your body have died and replicated. The death that imprisoned humanity was far less dramatic than a violent death, but also far more pervasive than merely imposing a time-limit on the beating of our hearts.

One of the greatest theologians in Christianity, Athanasius of Alexandria, described at the beginning of the 4th century what had been happening to humanity since the Fall, which he calls "the Transgression." He writes, "Death and corruption were gaining ever firmer hold on them, the human race was in the process of destruction. Man, who was created in God's image and in his possession of reason reflected the very Word Himself, was disappearing, and the work of God was being undone. The law of death, which followed from the Transgression, prevailed upon us, and from it there was no escape."[64]

Like a virus, sin infected humanity with a fatal disease that would not only kill us as individuals, but then be passed

---

[64] Athanasius. *On the Incarnation.* Circa 313 CE

down through our DNA to every subsequent generation. Without a cure, humanity itself would suffer a gradual decay until the day that we disappeared entirely.

Death became the enemy that would undo all that God lovingly created.

Act II: Pursuit

The history of humanity as told by the Christian faith admittedly goes from good news to bad news in a hurry. This of course is not God's fault, but only our own.

Fortunately for humanity, Saint Paul encourages us in 1 Corinthians 13 when he says that love "always protects, always trusts, always hopes, and always perseveres." The Christian faith is ultimately one of good news, not the least of which is because God perseveres to rescue us out of what seems to be a hopelessly bad situation. Broken relationships, injustice to our neighbor, corruption of our earth, and death to ourselves are emphatically *not* the permanent trajectory of humanity.

God brings us good news out of bad news. God brings us what the Christian faith calls *the gospel*.[65] It's a story about God coming to our rescue.

The fullness of this gospel, however, needed time to develop. Apart from hitting some sort of divine reset-button that would utterly wipe out human freedom, the pervasiveness of sin could not be undone by God casually letting us off with a verbal warning or handing out a get-out-of-jail-free card. The kind of rescue that was necessary could not be undertaken until sufficient events in human history transpired.

Civilization had to develop enough where the good news of reconciliation between God and humanity could be

---

[65] From the Old English word *godspel,* meaning "good news."

transmitted transnationally and transculturally, while at the same time the people group[66] that this rescue would emanate from had to develop a conceptual framework that could help them actually make sense of what God was doing. If God's plan was implemented before the technology existed to share it, the news would remain stuck in a single ethnicity and culture. If rescue came before a sophisticated monotheism developed, no one would be able to grasp the news.[67]

As civilization evolved technologically over thousands of years, God was preparing the Hebrew people theologically for what God was going to do at the ideal time.

Proto-Gospels

Almost as soon as humanity could doom itself to the effects of estrangement, God signaled that there was a plan to reconcile us back to Godself. No sooner than God pronouncing the bad news of estrangement on Adam and Eve does God provide the first *proto-gospel*. If the gospel message of the Christian faith is like a feature film, a proto-gospel is like the film's trailer. It's a symbol, often subtle and peculiar, that foreshadows in a small way what God will do one day in the grandest way.

The first proto-gospel is found in Genesis 3, where God says a descendent of humanity will crush the serpent's head. The serpent, we remember, is a symbol of the Adversary and forces bent on stealing, killing, and destroying all the good in the world. Somehow – and the story doesn't say how – a descendent of humanity, a "son of man," will successfully free us from the prison of sin that humanity locked itself up in.

---

[66] Defined by sociologists as a groups of individuals, families and clans who share a common language and ethnic identity.
[67] Hebrew religion did not even begin as monotheism, but as "monolatry," or the fidelity to a single god over other gods. Eventually, the Hebrews realized their Yahweh-God was the only God.

That is only the first proto-gospel though. These archetypes are buried all over the Hebrew texts. Still, in Genesis 3, before Adam and Eve are forced out of the garden for their sin, God kills the first animal recorded in the Bible, using its skin to cover humanity. It's not a perfect covering, but it's better than our attempt at sewing fig leaves together, and it again alludes to what God will do for us. A bloody sacrifice will somehow – the story doesn't say how – be provided by God that will cover our shame and guilt caused by sin.

Later, in Genesis 9, the Hebrew sages retell the Gilgamesh flood myth as a last-resort decision by God to reluctantly hold back the growing evil in the world with a catastrophic flood. In our English translations, the ending of this story then reveals that God places a rainbow in the sky as a sign that God, in stark contrast to the temperamental pagan deities, will never execute this kind of annihilating justice on humanity again. This would appear to be an unconnected symbol for such a promise, but in the original Hebrew language it doesn't read that God placed a *rainbow* in the sky. Instead, God placed over our heads the Hebrew word for *war bow*. This symbolic weapon of God's justice hung above humanity and aimed not downward towards earth, but upwards towards Heaven. God wasn't relenting on his justice against sin but somehow – the story doesn't say how – God will provide a way to administer justice against sin without punishing sinners.

In Genesis 22, God asks a man named Abraham to sacrifice his only son to God. Abraham came from a pagan culture that sacrificed children, so God's request does not seem to surprise him. He takes his only son up a hill to make this agonizing sacrifice on the pretense of a ceremony to worship God. His son wonders aloud where the sacrificial lamb is, but dutifully carries the very firewood on his back that he will be sacrificed on. When Abraham is about to kill his son, God stops him. This God is different than the other gods. There will be no human sacrifices in this new faith, and yet God does not abolish sacrifice entirely.

God provides an adult ram for Abraham to use, and sets in motion a religious tradition of sacrificing lambs and goats for the forgiveness of sin. The practice of animal sacrifice was meant to be offensive, to shock us out of our rationalizations of sin and our tendency to sanitize its hideousness. It was a gruesome reminder that sin leads to death, and that forgiveness can be costly. The Hebrews knew that the animal life couldn't truly and fully forgive the damage human lives had wrought, but it represented a hope that something truly could. Again, somehow, God was going to provide a sacrifice to end all sacrifices.

All these proto-gospels are simply some of the ones found in the *first* book of the Bible.

Whether or not these stories represent completely accurate historical events or completely allegorical tales is not very consequential to the historicity of Christianity. So why do they matter? To have faith in the past about these proto-gospels is to believe they are not merely an endless string of literary coincidences. These stories were told and written down a thousand years before the birth of Christ by people who had little or no conception of a savior that would one day rescue them from the effects of estrangement from God.

This kind of foreshadowing is as beautiful as it is improbable, and yet the proto-gospels are proclaiming a mystery in front of our eyes. In fact, it is hard to adequately explain how they would come to be told and written if they *did not* foreshadow a greater work by God. To have faith in this past then is to acknowledge that since these stories were told long before Christ, we trust that God's Spirit was working behind and through them to point us to an historical event that would make sense of all these otherwise inexplicable vignettes.

Covenants

"I promise." Such a brief but weighty phrase. Few things are more valuable than a promise kept. Few things are more devastating than a promise broken.

As it turns out, the story of God and people is one of God keeping God's promises and people all too often breaking their promise. You and I might quickly tire of such a lopsided relationship dynamic. Yet God, persevering in love toward humanity out of a gracious nature that defies any human limit, continues to make new and better promises to us anyway. The Bible calls these sacred promises "covenants," and they are an important element in the history of Christian faith.

All of God's covenants begin with grace, in that they are undeserved gifts from God that we have not merited. Most scholars believe the covenants found in the Hebrew narratives imitated a blend of two kinds of ancient contracts: marriage oaths and vassal treaties. The marriage oaths reflected God's desire to restore loving relationship between divinity and humanity. It also meant that covenants, despite their list of conditions, were always less about obedience than they were about fidelity.

As for the vassal treaties, they reflected the kind of arrangement a great empire would make with a meager nation. In those scenarios, the empire unilaterally offered a promise to defend and look after the nation and the nation's people in turn promises loyalty and resources. Betrayal warranted death.

With both ancient inspirations, God's covenants were similar in terms of scale, but not nearly as transactional in scope. God's marital-style covenants always implied commitment *regardless* of whatever spiritual infidelity might be committed by the betrothed. Likewise, God didn't *need* the loyalty or resources of people, and vassal-style covenants were not conditionally set up in the way an empire would have set them up. It was not, "God will do X *if* you will do Y." It was always, "God *has done* X, so you shall do Y."

Why *shall* though? Isn't that a little demanding of God? Hardly, when you consider the arrangement. Whatever God asked of people paled in comparison to what God was doing on their behalf. As we have already seen, God didn't want human sacrifices. In fact, what God fundamentally required was to "practice justice, kindness, and humility." [68] The sacrifice God wanted the most was a "humble and repentant heart."[69] Loyalty to these requirements, and the resources that it might take to honor them, truly was a fitting response to the only being who could rightfully ask for them. God would in turn use those faithful people to bless others, administer justice, and display God's glory to the world.

Depending on which biblical scholar you ask, there are four to seven covenants identified in what Christians call the Old Testament.[70] There is one covenant, however, that stands out as central to all others called the *Abrahamic covenant*. This is the same Abraham that God demonstrated a proto-gospel to by substituting Abraham's son with a ram for a sacrificial death. Calling Abraham out of his pagan land, God promised Abraham this as recorded in Genesis 12:1-3:

> *"Go from your country and your kindred and your father's house to the land that I will show you. And I will make of you a great nation, and I will bless you and make your name great, so that you will be a blessing. I will bless those who bless you, and him who dishonors you I will curse, and in you all the families of the earth shall be blessed."*

---

[68] Micah 6:8
[69] Psalm 51:17
[70] Edenic/Adamic, Noahic, Abrahamic, Mosaic, Palestinian, Priestly, and Davidic.

There was nothing special about Abraham. He was not particularly moral, smart, or powerful. In fact, he wasn't really any of these things at all. Nevertheless, Abraham trusted God's promise. [71] His faith in God, though very limited, was considered sufficient by God to overcome estrangement and enter into a renewed relationship. Even better, this sacred promise of blessing, relationship, and salvation by God will be the promise that follows Abraham's descendants for generations, no matter how badly they fail to love and obey God.

There is another surprising side effect of this covenant. Abraham is blessed, not to exclusion of others, or even for his own sake, but specifically for the sake of blessing others. The promise God makes to Abraham is not just for Abraham and those related to him. It is for all the families of the earth. This means even pagans can be blessed and saved by God. If we were to read on, we would find Abraham's descendent Joseph saves the pagan Egyptians from a famine later in the Genesis narrative.

God's expansion of blessings becomes even more radical once Abraham's descendants become the nation of Israel hundreds of years later. Most notably, in the Book of 2 Kings, we discover shocking story about a pagan Syrian commander named Naaman. This pagan is not only healed, but also converted by his encounter with God, and yet, Naaman doesn't join the religion of the Hebrews afterwards. He returns to his pagan homeland while continuing to enjoy the blessings of his healing and newfound relationship with this God who wants to bless all families of the earth. [72]

---

[71] For those concerned about God's "curse," this should be understood as an injunction against revenge. God, not us, will be the agent of any punishment, whereas God's people are to be the agents of blessing.

[72] 2 Kings 5:1-19

Why are covenants important for a Christian's faith in the past, especially the Abrahamic covenant? Covenants were the overarching idea that held the diverse and messy Hebrew narratives together. The Hebrew people, for the most part, did not understand the proto-gospels in the way Christians do. Since proto-gospels can really only be made sense of once we encounter *the* gospel in which they all point to, they primarily serve as a retroactive reference points proving God had been at work all along.

Covenants, on the other hand, were an explicit and continual point of reference for the Hebrew people and the formal Jewish faith that later emerged. They were *a people of the covenant*. By *people*, it meant that God did not call just special individuals, but entire communities. No one was exempt from its responsibilities or excluded from its blessings. By *of the covenant*, it meant that God was dealing with people primarily out of grace.

Without a covenant, God's blessings, relationship, and salvation would still be conditional on their performance. Without a covenant, the Hebrews couldn't even be sure if God wanted to provide anything good to them at all. Covenants, particularly the Abrahamic covenant, were the assurance that God never gives up on God's people, and that God's plan truly was to reconcile the whole world to Godself.

Better still, since God's promise to Abraham was given without an expiration date, we are to understand it is a promise still honored by God today. To have faith in this history grafts even those of the Christian faith thousands of years later into being part of the covenant people too.

Prophets

As brilliantly haunting as some proto-gospels are, God didn't just provide literary archetypes pointing God's people to a future hope and reality. Covenants did provide assurance of God's commitment to God's people, but the Bible tells an embarrassingly consistent tale of our individual and collective ability to break our promises to God. To graciously accommodate these failures, God also sent to the Hebrew people what the Bible calls prophets. Their stories are recorded in books of the Bible that often bear their name, sometimes dictated by the prophets themselves or compiled from oral tradition in the generation or two after their deaths.

Contrary to popular imagination, prophets didn't predict the future so much as tell the truth about God's will. They often showed up to call God's people back to covenantal faithfulness, to essentially renew their spiritual marriage vows. This self-critical orientation, rather than judging those outside the faith, has shaped faithful Christians' spiritual posture to this day.

While a Hebrew man named Moses is considered the original prophet and predates the founding of Israel, from approximately 1000 BCE to 420 BCE prophets were typically, ordinary men and women called by God to extraordinary works on behalf of God. While some of the bold preaching truth-to-power stories or records of their miraculous acts are impressive, all of the prophets suffered deeply in some form or another. From blinding pride, deep spiritual doubt, embarrassing cowardice, or even suicidal depression, [73] the prophetic calling of God was understandably resisted by those it came upon. It didn't help that prophets were rarely, if ever, popular with the people they were sent to.

Like the proto-gospels and covenants, there are too many prophets to cover in our brief discussion on what it means to have an historic faith. Nevertheless, it is important to believe in the historicity of the prophets for two reasons. First,

---

[73] Num. 20:1-14; Exod. 4:1-13; Judg. 6:11-24; Luke 1:13-20; Hab. 1:1-4; Jer. 1:1-6; 1 Kings 19:1-4; Exod. 5:17-23

the prophets teach us about God's character toward those who trust God. We can speak with confidence about what and who God is not simply out of our personal preferences, but because we have witnessed God through the life of the prophets, demonstrating God's character. Second, the prophets, in similarity to the proto-gospels, provide figures of the past that will be repeated in the future by God. This is called a *typology*. We should look for the combined attributes of the many prophets to be bound up in a single savior. To help flesh this out, let us highlight just a few different types of prophets and the typologies they embody.

Moses was the first prophet in the Hebrew narratives and is found in the Book of Exodus. He is known for delivering the enslaved Hebrew people from the clutches of the Egyptians, handing down the famous Ten Commandments, and leading his people to freedom in the "promised land" of what became Israel.[74]

The life of Moses teaches us that God hears the cries of those who are oppressed, never forgets about us even when it feels like God might have, and is incredibly patient with us. As a figure pointing to what God will do in the future, we can anticipate that God will deliver a much larger group of people from a form of slavery, hand down new commandments to them, and lead this new people into freedom.

The prophets did not just fulfill roles as spiritual leaders or generals. Some functioned as subversive individuals that hardly anyone followed. Hosea was a prophet around the eighth century BCE who gave messages of judgment and destruction upon Israel, which did nothing to help his popularity. Hosea, however, was fully committed to his message in a way that we would find scandalous. Inspired by God's prompting, Hosea married a prostitute who would

---

[74] Exodus 14, 20:1-17; Joshua 1:12-15

continually scorn his affection and lapse again and again into infidelity. Even their children bore names that were meant to remind the people of Israel of God's coming judgment.[75]

What was this supposed to teach us? Hosea was demonstrating how God is the scorned lover, but that even in our spiritual infidelity God will pursue us. Our estrangement, as tragic as it may be at times, does not need to be permanent. Pointing to the future, God will also one day redeem his people from our promiscuity with callous idols. God's exclusive love will be sufficient to win our hearts.

Still, other prophets did serve to tell of the future in a way that did not necessarily provide timetables written in stone, but rather a solid hope for the future of the Hebrew people in the midst of suffering. Jeremiah, who foretold and then witnessed firsthand the destruction of Jerusalem in the sixth century BCE, also predicted a return to freedom. That freedom, however, would take generations. In the meantime, God wanted the captive Jewish people to work to bless their conqueror's capital city that they now found themselves in. Jeremiah assured them that God, despite their assumptions about God's limitations, was working through even pagan nations.[76]

Jeremiah's prophecies show us that God is not only sovereign over everything, but even in the wake of tragedies, God is capable of redeeming those tragedies for good and beautiful purposes. God also used Jeremiah to give one of the many prophecies that pointed to a day where God was going to come and do something astounding among God's people and in the world.

---

[75] Hosea 1:1-11, Lo-Rahamah and Lo-Ammi, which mean "Not Loved" and "Not My People."
[76] Jeremiah 29:4-7

31 "Behold, the days are coming, declares the LORD, when I will make a new covenant with the house of Israel and the house of Judah, 32 not like the covenant that I made with their fathers on the day when I took them by the hand to bring them out of the land of Egypt, my covenant that they broke, though I was their husband, declares the LORD. 33 For this is the covenant that I will make with the house of Israel after those days, declares the LORD: I will put my law within them, and I will write it on their hearts. And I will be their God, and they shall be my people. 34 And no longer shall each one teach his neighbor and each his brother, saying, 'Know the LORD,' for they shall all know me, from the least of them to the greatest, declares the LORD. For I will forgive their iniquity, and I will remember their sin no more." (Jeremiah 31:31-34)

The proto-gospels, if but blurry gleams of the glory to come, were now starting to come into focus. The covenants, as gracious as they were, were about to be renewed with a covenant so amazing there would never be a need for another. As a result, there began to emerge an expectation that God would send a savior, or messiah, to the Jewish people. Some kind of revolutionary man would fulfill all of the grand hopes proclaimed by the prophets

Why is this so crucial to our understanding of Christianity? It's an important piece of evidence that the hope of God coming to rescue people wasn't a fanciful ad hoc idea by the early Christians. It was a long-awaited promise that was expected to be kept. To have faith in the past is to trust that the Hebrew prophets were calling God's people back to keep their sacred promises even as God was preparing them for a revolutionary new one. When we place ourselves into these stories, it prepares our own hearts for its fulfillment.

CHAPTER FOUR Faith In The Past

Act III: Reconciliation

Fulfillment of the grandest hopes about salvation came in the humblest of ways; a helpless infant was born to an impoverished teenage mom in the backwater town of a backwater region under the heel of an empire that didn't care if its subjects lived or died, so long as they paid their taxes.[77]

This was not the expectation. God's great saving act, the decisive intervention into human history, was supposed to be more impressive than that. Which, of course, is why I think this story must be true.

If we were making this up, if this was a fable that reflected our anthropomorphic fantasies, God's messianic work should have looked like typical human expectations and typical human agendas. A brave general would have been selected by God to lead a physical army against evil nations. This was, in fact, the expectation of many Jewish religious leaders at the time. They believed that God was going to send a king to rule in the legacy of their royal line. This king was expected to be a warrior and a ruler, a general and a politician. This savior would defeat the evil Romans, the most recent subjugator of the Jewish people.

The mistake though, was not in being too literal about the words of prophets, but in being too provincial. The scope of their hope was too limited. The evil that God intended to

---

[77] Luke 2:1-20, Sven Günther, "Taxation in the Greco-Roman World: The Roman Principate," *Oxford Handbooks*, Oxford University Press (April 2016).

defeat was not merely political. As we have so often witnessed at home and abroad, despite all the grandiose slogans of new leaders promising change, much like a parasite, evil only seems to find new hosts. God's war was also not with any nation. Though we like to cast the blame outward, our central human dilemma has never been outside of ourselves, but instead nests in our very hearts. Lest all of humanity die, we cannot kill the problem away.

The ancient Jewish prophecies that looked forward to a savior were never about God parachuting in with a plan of regime change. God was invading the whole earth to reconcile its people from their estrangement to God.

The Arrival of God

The divine invasion commenced with what the Christian faith calls the *incarnation of God.*

God did not arrive on earth in terrifying power to justly crush humanity for our explicit and complicit evils, but chose to become humanity and suffer evil and injustice alongside us in solidarity.[78]

God did this through the second personality of the Trinity, that is, the Son or Redeemer. The Triune God was emptied of divine privilege and power, and became fully human. This human was named Jesus, which means "Savior." Born between 6 BCE and 4 BCE in the tiny village of Bethlehem, Jesus grew up in the equally insignificant town of Nazareth. The Roman Empire – with its advanced paved highway system, religious pluralism, and savage militaristic efficiency – ruled here with an unusually light touch without relenting from its threatening glare.

---

[78] John 3:17

Jesus was known to his contemporaries as "Jesus of Nazareth."[79] Sometimes he referred to himself as "The Son of God,"[80] alluding to his divine intimacy with his Heavenly Father. More often though, Jesus referred to himself as "The Son of Man,"[81] alluding to both a Jewish prophecy and to demonstrate God's unreserved solidarity with the human experience. His disciples would later call him "Jesus Christ,"[82] since "Christ" meant "The Anointed One" or "Messiah."

Jesus, or Christ, is referenced by a handful of first-century Roman and Jewish historians, as well as Jewish religious documents compiled in the following centuries.[83] These documents typically contain a few dismissive lines of commentary about Jesus and his followers, but altogether they show that he was a genuine historical figure who was both executed by the government and revered as divine by the first Christians. Beyond those rudimentary sources, what informs Christian beliefs about Jesus are four historical accounts in the Bible that tell the story of Jesus, each with their own themes, timeline, and cultural focus. Not to be confused with *the* gospel message, these accounts are called the gospels according to Mark, Matthew, Luke and John respectively. All of them were written approximately between 55 and 95 CE.

In the two accounts about the life of Jesus that contain details of his childhood, he is born of a virgin named Mary. The Christian faith has always held that Jesus was born of a virgin, as proof of his divine origins and a fulfillment of a prophecy found in the Book of Isaiah.[84] This declaration made its way into the first official statement of beliefs by the Church,

---

[79] Luke 18:37; John 19:19
[80] Luke 22:70; John 5:25
[81] Mark 10:45; Matthew 9:6; Luke 9:26; John 6:53
[82] Acts 2:38; Romans 5:1; 1 Peter 1:3
[83] See Tacitus, Pliny the Younger, Josephus, Lucian, the Jerusalem Talmud, and the Babylonian Talmud.
[84] Isaiah 7:14

the *Nicene Creed*, in the fourth century. However, the virgin birth has been met with no shortage of incredulity since the early twentieth century. Apart from its miraculous nature, it has been pointed out that based on the interpretive flexibility of the Hebrew word in the prophecy about the Messiah's birth, "virgin" could also be translated to mean "young woman."

It's often been asked if the doctrine of the virgin birth is required in order to be a genuine Christian. In one sense, it's not. If Jesus was not born of a virgin, it would not necessitate his loss of divinity. It's reasonable to imagine that God does not metaphysically require a virgin birth to incarnate Godself into human form. That said, for anyone willing to seriously consider Christianity, the skepticism around the virgin birth seems misplaced.

If the Christian faith believes in a God who became fully human and literally *rose from the dead*, why would one have any problem believing in something as relatively easy as a virgin birth? Nothing comes back from death, but virgin births have recently been well-documented among multiple animal species in a phenomenon known as parthenogenesis.[85] While parthenogenesis in a human would still be a miracle, it would be one of a lesser degree than a resurrection of a dead entombed body.

Regardless, it only seems fitting that from birth to death, and even beyond death, a story about the God-Man *should* be distinguished by miracles. Jesus artfully defied the claims of illegitimacy in birth and made the claims of death illegitimate.

It is perhaps more surprising that so little is known about Jesus' early life. There is only one story recorded of Jesus when he was a boy, and one that reveals his incredible spiritual

---

[85] Sylvia Pagán Westphal, "'Virgin Birth' Mammal Rewrites Rules of Biology," *New Scientist*, April 21, 2004.

insight and closeness to the God he called "Father."[86] However, like every other human being, Jesus had to grow in knowledge and spiritual wisdom by reading and absorbing the Jewish scriptures. The biblical accounts give no indication he was born knowing his divine mission nor his divine status. We do not know when he realized that he was not just human, but also the incarnated Triune God. Only by an ever-deepening faith and interpreting the ancient prophecies pertaining to the Messiah in a way no one else ever had, does Jesus eventually become aware that his mission was to accomplish the rescue of humanity by his life, death, and resurrection.

With that awareness, Jesus began his public ministry around age thirty as an itinerant *rabbi*, or Jewish teacher. His cousin and Judaism's foremost prophetic figure at the time, a man known as John the Baptist, publicly endorsed Jesus as the one John existed to point others toward. Recalling what God did for Abraham and the animal sacrificial system practiced by Judaism, at the sight of Jesus approaching the Jordan river John announced, "Behold, the Lamb of God, who takes away the sin of the world!"[87] The Jesus movement had begun.

Contrary to what you may have heard, Jesus did not primarily teach about how to reach Heaven. Though Heaven did certainly factor in, Jesus' self-declared emphasis was on a new reality much more immediate than a place to go one day when you die. Jesus proclaimed and invited his listeners to participate in what he called the *"The Kingdom of God."*[88] This new God-initiated plan for human flourishing was in marked contrast, if not outright opposition, to the governments of humanity. In fact, nearly every description that Jesus gave about the Kingdom of God is told with countercultural twists.

---

[86] Luke 2:41-52
[87] John 1:29
[88] Or "Kingdom of Heaven" as told in the Jewish-sensitive Gospel of Matthew. These phrases are generally considered interchangeable in meaning.

The Kingdom of God will humble the proud and honor the humble, overthrow the oppressors and free the oppressed, and take back from the rich and give their inheritance to the poor. In the parables Jesus uses to teach about what the Kingdom of God is like, its heroes are society's left-outs.[89]

Roughly half of Jesus' recorded encounters were with people that first-century Jewish religious leaders would have spoken with only to condemn. Prostitutes, heretics, occupying soldiers, treacherous collaborators, and ethnic enemies are counted among his friends and followers.[90] The other half of those encounters were often escalating debates with the religious establishment. The Kingdom of God, both distinctly Jewish and yet existing beyond any specific religion, was a shockingly open way of approaching God and a radically gracious way for relating to people.

The Kingdom of God was not only a way of living, but also a proclamation about a new event in human history. From then on, Jesus would say, "The Kingdom of God is in the midst of you."[91] God was now interacting with humanity in an unprecedented way, a way that the prophets from ages past had looked forward to but never experienced like this. Like an ancient Roman herald who brought to a town the *evangelion,* literally the "good news" of a victorious general or liberating king, Jesus proclaimed a divine *evangelion* in a way that was unmistakable to his audience.

This is not to say Jesus didn't proclaim spiritual salvation. He certainly did, though there is an important nuance to be made. The spiritual salvation that Jesus provided and that the Christian faith proclaims is much more the result of the penultimate action of Jesus rather than his teachings. If we were to summarize the theme of Jesus' teachings, we would

---

[89] Matthew 5:3,10, 19:21, 22:1-14
[90] Luke 7:36-50; Mark 2:15-17; John 8:1-11
[91] Luke 17:21

not find so much about getting to Heaven from earth as how to unleash Heaven on earth.

Yet did Jesus proclaim that he was, in fact, God? It is one thing to teach people how to follow God. It is another thing altogether to teach people to follow *you* as God. The former could be said of Moses or Muhammad in Western religion, or Gautama Buddha, Confucius, or the gurus in Eastern religion. The latter could be said of residents in the psychiatric ward and cult leaders who commit mass suicide.

Some scholars critical of Christianity have pointed out that Jesus never says in a way our English language could directly translate, "I am God." While this is true, such a statement would have been too easily accepted and misunderstood by polytheistic pagans. Jesus as just another deity in the pantheon of gods could have been a digestible – and wholly wrong – proposition. This language would have also contradicted the strict monotheism of Judaism and the later Trinitarian monotheism of Christianity. If Jesus had crudely said, "I am God" as an isolated claim, it would have implied God was currently on earth but not in Heaven. The Son was not the Father abandoning Heaven for a foray on earth, but one personality of the Triune God living among us while the rest of the universe was still held in the hands of the Father.

In fact, what Jesus says and does makes his claim to divinity with the monotheistic God of Israel unavoidable. In the Gospel of John, Jesus repeatedly declares that he is, "*I am*" in relationship to his Father in Heaven. [92] Why is this so meaningful? When Moses, staring at a burning bush that would not be consumed, asked God what he should tell people his name was, God answered, "I Am Who I Am." [93] This became one of the most important holy names of the Jewish

---

[92] John 8:58
[93] Exodus 3:14

God. The Jewish philosopher Philo, a contemporary of Jesus, also called God simply, "I Am." The author of John's gospel uses precisely the same Greek phrase when Jesus identifies himself.

While Saint John has been accused by skeptics of being overly-enthusiastic about Jesus' divinity, his perception of Jesus as God is reinforced by every other gospel account. Even in the Gospel of Mark, the most concise and unadorned telling of Jesus' life that also focuses the least on his divinity, still makes poetic references to his divinity on nearly every page. Assuming the prerogatives that were understood to be reserved for God alone, Jesus displayed divine power over healing, curing fatal illnesses, overcoming demonic forces, controlling weather, manipulating molecular structures, choreographing space-time, and conquering death itself. Jesus also forgives sins, which infuriated the local religious elites, since every Jew knew "that only God can forgive sins."[94] Again, this is all simply in the barebones account of Mark. Jesus' statements and actions that directly associate him with the One True God of Israel only grow stronger in the more detailed accounts by Matthew and Luke.

Jesus, in any account of his life, clearly claimed supernatural oneness with the God of Jewish monotheism.

The Death of God

A message that proclaims a new kingdom greater than any earthly kingdom, promises the overthrow of oppressive social systems, and upends religious intermediaries to directly commune with God, is the kind of message that will be threatening to supporters of the status quo. Claiming divine authority and identity could only add to the polarization of forces swirling around Jesus' movement.

---

[94] Mark 2:1-12

Very early in Jesus' ministry, religious leaders in the Judean countryside determined Jesus was a threat to their religious doctrine. Later, in Jerusalem, the religious leaders who oversaw the temple system determined Jesus was a threat to the entire political establishment. Once Jesus was identified as both a religious and political liability, his murder was a foregone conclusion. God was offering life in the Kingdom of God through the Son of God. Humanity instead demanded his death.

As Jesus ate what he knew would be his final meal with his disciples, he instituted an essential Christian practice called the *Eucharist* or *The Lord's Supper* or *Communion*. This basic Jewish meal mirrored what was about to happen. His body would be broken like bread and his blood poured out like wine. Jesus told his disciples it was also a covenant, a new covenant that drew together all the ancient promises of God somehow fulfilled by the very breaking of his body and the pouring out of his blood.

Shortly after, in a nearby garden just outside of Jerusalem, security forces dispatched by the Jewish temple's religious leadership, the Sanhedrin, arrested the revolutionary rabbi. This was likely done with permission from the occupying Roman authorities as well. The Sanhedrin was tipped off by one of the twelve disciples who had grown disillusioned with Jesus' message. Judas Iscariot, who had likely longed for a violent overthrow of the Roman occupation, colluded with the Sanhedrin to arrange the trap in hopes that it would force Jesus to fight back and ignite a Jewish revolt.[95] In his apprehension, Jesus' disciples either fled or tried to fight to prevent his capture, but Jesus ordered them to stand down.[96]

---

[95] "Iscariot" may have been taken from the "Sicarii," a militant Jewish militant group that was destroyed in 70 CE. This would also explain Judas' suicidal remorse at Jesus' "unintentional" death.

[96] John 18:1-11

The security forces bound and took Jesus to the nearest military barracks.

Jesus did not surrender to the authorities because he thought he would receive a fair trial. He knew what was coming next, mockery, abuse, torture, and execution. This fate, however, was the very reason God incarnated Godself in the man, Jesus of Nazareth. God's ultimate purpose was not merely showing people a code of ethics to live by, but achieving a means for people to live forever. How? Jesus tells his disciples, by "giv[ing] his life as a ransom for many."[97] From the beginning of his ministry, Jesus knew he was headed for death, and it was meant to be a death that would somehow save others.

Tried by a seething kangaroo court in the pitch-black hours sometime after midnight, the court sentenced Jesus to death for blasphemy, for claiming divine authority to change the existing religious system.[98] This charge though was not enough to merit state-sponsored execution, since the Romans cared little for internal Jewish squabbles. The Sanhedrin and those allies who stood to benefit from killing Jesus, attempted to persuade the Roman governor, Pontius Pilate, that Jesus was attempting to organize an insurrection. Jesus was, after all, gaining followers for a Kingdom of God.[99]

By every gospel account, Pilate seems unconvinced by these allegations. Pilate, however, was neither interested in protecting the innocent nor cared about protecting Jewish religious doctrine. All that mattered to the Roman governor was keeping political order and preventing riots by his conquered subjects. In fact, his failure to do so a few years later would lead to his recall to Rome to stand trial for cruelty and violation of Roman due-process laws. So, with the threat of a

---

[97] Mark 10:45
[98] Mark 14:53-65
[99] John 19:12

riot on his hands by Jesus' politically well-connected accusers and since he likely deduced that Jesus' outcast followers seemed less prone to violence, Pilate signed off on the sentence of execution for the alleged "King of the Jews."[100]

Jesus of Nazareth, after a nearly fatal flogging and carrying his own hundred-pound crossbar to the outskirts of Jerusalem, was crucified on a Roman cross on a hill called Golgotha. Crucifixion was such a horrible death that women and Roman citizens were protected from it by law. Conquered subjects, especially insurrectionists, were not. Two men, likely Jewish rebels, were crucified to the right and left of Jesus. The soldiers posted a sign above Jesus' head that read in three languages, "King of the Jews." Using the languages of religion (Hebrew), culture (Greek), and politics (Latin), the Roman overlords did not want anyone to be confused about why this Jewish rabbi was slowly succumbing to such a gruesome fate.[101]

Hanging on the cross, it took about nine hours for the Son of Man to die. Death was accelerated by the blood loss he suffered in his flogging. John's gospel records that when a Roman centurion attempted to confirm Jesus' death by piercing his lungs with a spear, blood and water poured out. Saint John, writing down only what was reported to him, misidentified the fluid as water. Instead, the water was really pleural effusion, a fluid buildup in the lungs brought on from the strain of Jesus instinctively attempting to hold himself up on the cross in an effort to prevent suffocation.[102]

This strain also would have caused pericardial effusion, creating enormous pressure on his heart. Given that the gospel accounts uniformly describe Jesus as anticipating the moment of his death, it is likely his specific cause of death was a heart attack. The Son of God died of a broken heart.

---

[100] Matt. 27:24-26
[101] John 19:17, 20; Matt. 27:37-38
[102] John 19:34

Up until this point, little of what happened to Jesus – from the standpoint of human history – was unusual. The powerful sought to preserve their control by any means necessary. Court systems failed to administer justice. Soldiers slaughtered rebellious subjects with efficient cruelty. Jesus' death, as tragic as it was, is remarkably standard from a callous, historical point of view. However, the story then takes a seemingly unimportant, but unusual turn. Most dead criminals would have been dumped into a common grave, their bodies picked apart by scavenging birds and wild dogs.

The deviation from convention is that all four gospel writers record that there was a sympathizer of Jesus, Joseph of Arimathea, who sat on the temple council that sentenced Jesus to death, but who was left out of the pre-dawn trial. Leveraging his political privilege for good, Joseph of Arimathea offered his family tomb for the deceased rabbi and the Roman authorities granted Joseph possession of the body. Hewn out of rock and protected by a massive stone cover, it was Friday evening when Jesus' corpse was wrapped according to Jewish tradition, laid in this wealthy man's tomb, and sealed inside.[103]

The Resurrection of God

By the time Jesus was buried on Friday, most of his closest disciples had scattered. They anticipated they might be next to suffer the same fate as accomplices to a failed revolt. In fact, the only disciples we know that stayed with Jesus until his tomb was sealed were the female disciples of Jesus and two Jewish religious leaders who were secret disciples.

We don't know what the disciples did on Saturday before regrouping in the room where they would spend the night. The gospel writers provide us with no details, though it's relatively safe to assume there were many tears and much hand

---

[103] Mark 15:42-47; Matt. 27:57-60; Luke 23:50-55; John 19:38-42

wringing. We are told in Matthew's account that a squad of Roman soldiers stood post outside Jesus' tomb to prevent the disciples from stealing his body. It was a wise strategic move by Pilate and the religious leaders, but also one that laughably overestimated the resolve of a group that previously fled simply at the sight of approaching soldiers.[104]

There is also scant biblical teaching about what was happening to Jesus during this time. Was he simply unconscious? Sitting around in Heaven? A book of the Bible attributed to Saint Peter – another of Jesus' closest disciples – answers this question, if ever so briefly.[105] Jesus went to the dead and proclaimed the good news. [106] Early Christians imagined Jesus conducting a rescue mission to a place similar to the Greek idea of Hades or the Roman Catholic idea of limbo, where existence was neither paradise nor punishment. Though nowhere in the Bible does it mention anything about Jesus venturing to hell, historically this Saturday foray has been given the misnomer "The Harrowing of Hell." Regardless, it was a beloved image for artists in the Early and Medieval Church, with iconography of Jesus plucking a haggard Adam and Eve out from a shattered grave. Dante makes reference to it in his classic, *Inferno*, where Hell still bears the meteoric scars of Christ cratering down through it. In other words, Jesus made use of his death just as much as his life to proclaim liberation to the captives.

This was, of course, all unbeknownst to the mourning disciples. From their perspective, their beloved rabbi was dead, and any messianic hopes they had were crucified with him. Some disciples already had begun to head home to their old lives to pick up the pieces of whatever they had left behind.

---

[104] Matt. 27:62-66
[105] Peter could have been told this by Jesus after his resurrection. More likely, he received a Spirit-given dream of it much later, as he did in the Book of Acts 10:9-16.
[106] 1 Pet. 3:18-20; 1 Pet. 4:6

Others huddled together in an upper room in Jerusalem consoling one another and attempting to figure out what to do next. There were no good options.

Sunday morning came. Some of the female disciples – the gospel accounts vary in the precise names and number even though all agree that Mary Magdalene was present – thought it a good idea to bring some spice preservatives to apply to Jesus' hastily wrapped corpse. It was a sincere, if likely futile, coping mechanism for their grief. If there were guards at the tomb, would they let them pass? Could they even open a stone tomb designed to be shut permanently? Doing something though was better than not doing anything. The women trudged on past the twilight hour towards the tomb. When they arrived, nothing was as it should have been – or at least not as they expected.

The battle-hardened Roman soldiers were nowhere to be found. The stone entrance to the tomb was rolled away. Inside, grave clothes were lain as if collapsed over air. There was no corpse.

Jesus had been resurrected from the dead.[107]

The gospel accounts differ in some of the extraneous details regarding the next few moments. Mark records there was an angel present, while Matthew and Luke make it two angels, and John mentions disguised angels, perhaps to maintain a level of narrative suspense. However, all are unanimous in recording that the tomb that held Jesus' dead body was empty on Sunday morning, and that there was a proclamation that Jesus was alive – either by an angelic host or Jesus himself. Jesus would then appear to his disciples over a period of forty days, encouraging them, teaching them, and restoring their faith. Lastly, though it is implied by the other three gospels, Luke's gospel explicitly records Jesus

---

[107] Luke 24:1-8

transmitting himself from our earthly dimension to the dimension of Heaven, in what is known to the Christian faith as the *ascension*.[108]

Why did Jesus leave the world? Would it not have been more helpful to stick around? Perhaps in the short term it would have been helpful, but God endlessly walking around in human form was never the ultimate plan. The night of his arrest, Jesus told his disciples he would "prepare a place for [us]" in Heaven. He assured them he would be bringing us there himself by going before us. After his resurrection, Jesus also told his disciple Mary Magdalene, "I am ascending to my Father."[109] The perfect harmonious community, separated by the incarnation, needed to be restored. Convinced by these final recorded words of Jesus and by the corroborating descriptions from New Testament authors, [110] Christians believe that Jesus remains alive even now, reigning in Heaven as the victorious Son of God and reunited with the other personalities of the Trinity.

The Reliability of the Story

Volumes of books have been devoted to making credible something as incredible as a resurrection, much of it painstakingly researched and sober-minded. Here however, is not the place to "prove" the resurrection of Jesus of Nazareth to a skeptical reader. Belief in the historicity of the resurrection itself is as much of a spiritual conversion as an intellectual one. There are two important details to these accounts worth noting though that nearly guarantee they are original and faithful retellings of eyewitness reports. These details do not prove the resurrection happened, but that the first Christians *believed*

---

[108] Luke 24:50-53; Acts 1:1-11
[109] John 20:17
[110] 1 Pet. 3:22; Eph. 1:20; Col. 3:1; Heb. 12:2; Phil. 3:20-21

the resurrection happened. One detail is what they all do not possess, and the other is what they all do possess.

None of these accounts have fantastic details, much less details of the resurrection itself. Myths always grow in grandeur the longer they go on, likely from a desire to tantalize their followers and impress potential converts. Later stories about Jesus from the second and third century, stories not placed in the Bible due to problems with their reliability, do exactly this. [111] The fact that no gospel account includes a description of the resurrection itself and provides only the barest details around the empty tomb, testifies to the raw authenticity of the stories. The gospel authors simply reported the most reliable material available, even though such an unadorned story at the time begged for specifics.

There is also an important detail included in all four gospel accounts. Female disciples are the first witnesses to the empty tomb and the resurrection. If one were inventing a story about a resurrection in the ancient world meant to persuade others and make converts, such a fabrication would put forward the most credible spokesmen to testify about a man rising from the dead. The female disciples might as well be the opposite of this requirement. They were uneducated, poor, and worst of all – women. In the unabashedly patriarchal first century, the testimony of a woman was not even admissible in the court of law. The only remotely plausible reason women would be recorded as the first witnesses of the empty tomb and the resurrection would be because the report originated with them. Meeting the historian's mark of authenticity known as the *criterion of embarrassment*, the gospel authors faithfully reported even the details of the resurrection that hurt their credibility with their target audience.

---

[111] For example, the apocryphal gospel of Peter or gospel of Bartholomew have some wild stuff.

Why though, did the resurrection, as opposed to Jesus' brilliant teachings, matter the most to Jesus' disciples and to the first Christians? What made this event so important for a first-century Jew? After all, while not as joyful as the gospels' accounts and probably not even known by the earliest Christians, there were other ancient Greek and Egyptian legends that had deities coming back from the dead. What made this so different? There are two main reasons.

First, the resurrection was not a much-anticipated miracle that was easily believed by hopeful disciples. The Jewish disciples had no religious or philosophical category for the resurrection of a single person. First-century Jews, if they believed in a resurrection at all, anticipated a world-wide resurrection in the final judgment of God at the end of time. As radical as Jesus' teachings were, they were in most ways extensions of a Jewish worldview. The resurrection of Jesus was completely outside their religious imagination, and therefore signaled that something of supreme importance had occurred.

Second, the resurrection led to the opposite response one might expect from a God-Man who had just three days earlier, been abandoned by his friends and brutally murdered by his enemies. In the ancient Greek and Egyptian tales, any god that managed to come back from the dead did so to take revenge. Jesus rises from the dead and immediately appears to his fair-weather disciples bearing peace, blessings, and forgiveness.[112] God's plan of reconciliation was not thwarted by death. The resurrection, emerging from the shadow of the cross, was God's signatory stamp that God was truly reconciling all things to Godself.

---

[112] Luke 24:36-39

So What? Trusting God in Faith

For the Christian faith, the historicity of the life, death, and resurrection of God in the person of Jesus of Nazareth is the fulcrum upon which all of Christianity pivots. Until this point, belief in the literal history of the proto-gospels, covenants, or prophets has not been a prerequisite for essential Christian faith. Whether one understands them as literal events, allegorical retellings or some blend of both, what matters is that they point to a tangible reality. Yet a willingness to be comfortable with those interpretative differences can only be tenable *if* there is indeed an historical event connected to them. If allegories and biblical myths are like seeing through windows, we must genuinely see something solid through them. We cannot go on believing in endless allegories. The resurrection cannot be just another window.

This is why the life, death, and resurrection of God must be understood literally. We have faith that it is a true history that validates all the allegories. This is also an act of trust. If trusting that I am not God is a faith in a negative, trusting that God truly reconciled the world in linear time and physical space is a faith in the positive. Even if we might have an anxiety about a moment in the past that no one can return to verify with a contingent of modern reporters, unlike our primordial parents we choose to trust the sovereignty and goodness of God.

For if God did not incarnate Godself into humanity, if God was not executed by humanity, and if God was not raised from the dead in a resurrected human body, then the Christian faith collapses into mere optimism and sentimentalism. We become the purveyors of a dusty collection of well-meaning but ultimately meaningless morality tales. [113] We end up looking through windows forever, yet seeing nothing. The

---

[113] 1 Corinthians 15:12-14

literal presence of God in time and space gives substance and form to everything we hope is true.

Did the first Christians believe this though? Did they believe Jesus was resurrected? Could later Christians, perhaps under the sway of some crafty Roman emperor, have played up Jesus' influential ministry into miracles and his post-mortem appearances into a resurrection to elevate Jesus to a divine status? In a word, no.

The doctrines of the incarnation, Jesus' miracles, and the resurrection were well-established in the Early Church well before Christianity was legal in the Roman Empire, much less influenced by imperial politics. Bart Ehrman, perhaps the foremost skeptical historian and critic of Christianity, eventually concluded that, "It is indisputable that some of the followers of Jesus came to think that he had been raised from the dead, and that something had to have happened to make them think so."[114]

Ehrman, because he rejects the possibility of miracles, imagined the disciples independently experienced hallucinations of Jesus, or perhaps even genuine spiritual visions. For Ehrman though, either explanation would still be one side of the same, false coin. Despite the probability of such a scenario occurring bordering zero, this explanation also seems to avoid what the gospel accounts recount about the resurrected Jesus. They depict a transformed, but still entirely physical body. He can still be touched. He can still be conversed with normally. He can still have an appetite and eat. Even as the disciples grasp to understand how the resurrection of Jesus is even possible, there is no indication in any gospel account that any of them wonder if who they are interacting

---

[114] Bart D. Ehrman, *How Jesus Became God: The Exaltation of a Jewish Preacher from Galilee* (New York, NY: HarperOne, 2015), 183-184.

with is a ghost. Even if they did, Jesus explicitly assures them he is not.[115]

The disciples believed the resurrection because they were witnesses to the risen Christ. Trusting in their sensory perception, they believed because they saw. The Triune God invites us to trust Christ without that same advantage. Jesus tells his followers, "Blessed are those who have not seen and yet believe."[116] We are encouraged to trust God not on the reliability of what we may have seen or not seen, but ultimately on the reliability of God's character.

A Beautiful Story

The life, death, and resurrection of Jesus – if it is true – changed everything for the disciples in a way no ghostly vision or reverent memory ever could. It can do the same for us.

In every culture, in every place, and in every time, there have been stories told that are meant to explain humanity's fundamental dilemma, how to overcome it in this life, and an assurance of an ultimate resolution in the future. Those stories are filled with heroic figures, devout mystics, and brilliant sages. Some characters are meant to inspire us and teach us. Some perhaps are even said to be able to intercede from beyond the divide of death.

Yet nearly all of these religious stories, as wild and fascinating as they are, are myths. They spring up from the mists of time. They are once-upon-a-time. Even their adherents know better than to try to date them. This does not mean they are unimportant stories. To the contrary, even myths have the power to set our hearts on fire and lift our spirits. The ancient myths, whether from pagan religions or

---

[115] Luke 24:39-43; Acts 1:3
[116] John 20:29

Hebrew sages, all serve an even greater purpose. They are signposts for our souls.

The Oxford writer and professor, C.S. Lewis, loved Greek mythology. As a young intellectual who had firmly rejected Christianity during the horrors of trench warfare in the First World War, he grudgingly began to concede that the Christians he knew wrote better poetry than his atheist peers. Befriended by two fellow Christian professors, Hugo Dyson and J.R.R. Tolkien, the three academics would chat one night into early hours of the morning. Conversations of love, friendship and poetry eventually illuminated to Lewis a stunning meaning behind the world's myths. Lewis would later write to a friend,[117]

> *"Now what Dyson and Tolkien showed me was this: that if I met the idea of sacrifice in a Pagan story I didn't mind it at all: again, that if I met the idea of a god sacrificing himself to himself . . . I liked it very much and was mysteriously moved by it: again, that the idea of the dying and reviving god (Balder, Adonis, Bacchus) similarly moved me provided I met it anywhere except in the Gospels. The reason was that in Pagan stories I was prepared to feel the myth as profound and suggestive of meanings beyond my grasp even tho' I could not say in cold prose 'what it meant'."*

A world-altering realization came over Lewis. The Christianity he had rejected for so many years came into his field of spiritual vision, not as stale religiosity, but as the realized hope of a thousand myths. "The story of Christ is simply a true myth," Lewis concluded. "A myth working on us

---

[117] C.S. Lewis to Arthur Greeves, October 18, 1931, in Lewis, *Collected Letters*, vol. 1, 976.

in the same way as the others, but with this tremendous difference that it really happened."

We have all believed in myths. We may not have called them such, but we were captivated by their power all the same – the fairy tales, folk legends, comic books, or cinematic sagas. When we were children, we believed in magic. We did not necessarily believe because we thought the illusions were real, but because our hearts knew it gestured to a world that was. Right behind the curtain of the mundane and the dogmatically material, was a magical reality that peeked out and around and underneath the heavy veil.

It should give even the toughest skeptic a thoughtful pause that Christ-figures have not just haunted the modern world of literature and film, but that there are so many Christ-figures in ancient religions that knew nothing of Christ. They are never mirror images though of the gospel story. None lived, died, and resurrected like Christ. Their stories are not as glorious.

Still, their stories in piecemeal reflect glimmers of that glory. Some gods were born of virgins, or demonstrated great miracles, or came back to life after dying. Some religious teachers gave profound new teachings, or offered a path of salvation, or were martyred by evil forces. However, it is God in Christ alone that embodies the deepest human hopes in all the mythological gods and teachers. It is as if God was writing a universal human story that had to be first spun from the foreshadowing and precursors of every ancient religion.

The Bible says that all myths, all hopes, find their "yes" in Christ.[118]

This is not a story we can make up. This is a story we can only receive. Refined for ages and forged through countless cultures, we have been gifted a beautiful story meant

---

[118] 2 Corinthians 1:20

not for a singular era or people, but rightfully for the whole world. Christ, the true myth, is reconciling the world back to God.

CHAPTER FIVE
Love From Heaven

Little about the life and teachings of Jesus was understood before the death and resurrection of Jesus. If the death of Jesus crushed the spirits of his disciples, his resurrection restored them ten-fold. In the wake of this outcome that defied their wildest expectations and their previously held religious categories, the disciples were forced to ask, "So what now?"

The Book of Acts, a continuation of the Gospel of Luke, essentially begins with this question. Jesus ascends to Heaven and the disciples are left staring upward, mouths agape. Two angels have to jar them out of their dumbfounded stances, saying, "Men of Galilee, why do you stand looking into heaven? This Jesus, who was taken up from you into heaven, will come in the same way as you saw him go into heaven."[119]

Before Jesus' ascension, he commissioned the disciples as Apostles (or literally 'messengers') to pass on his teachings to every nation and to conduct the other essential Christian practice known as *baptism*, which is meant to picture a public identification with Jesus and the power of Christ to remove sin.

Apart from this mission, however, the newly minted Apostles are given few details by Jesus or any angel. With the inbound help of the third personality of the Trinity, the amorphous Holy Spirit, the Apostles must figure out how they will be faithful to Christ's commission between now and his return, of which he said no one will know the day or the hour.[120] What were these last three years with Jesus meant to show them?

They began to interpret the life of Jesus and the meaning of the Kingdom of God in a backwards approach. Backwards from the cross and resurrection, a whirlwind of epiphanies quickly followed. What they discovered is that the life, death, and resurrection of Jesus was a radical act of God's love. It was a love between the divine and humanity. It was *love from Heaven*.

God Enters Into Our Sin

The incarnation of God in the man Jesus of Nazareth was necessary for God to begin a process that would ultimately culminate in the resurrection of God. In light of that same resurrection, however, the earliest Christians began to realize that the incarnation of God was not merely a required step for God to move from heavenly point A to earthly point B. It was not even to provide us with new teachings that would guide the

---

[119] Acts 1:11
[120] Matthew 24:36

future followers of Jesus Christ. The incarnation was for God to participate in the fullness of the human experience.

There is something that feels unfair about a God who reigns in perfection up in Heaven and watches human life play out like a spectator at a sporting event. Not just a polite game of baseball either, but more like a rugby scrum where players can be maimed and murdered. This God creates all the rules for us, but never has to obey them. Sure, God is holy and perfect, but I imagine it would be much easier to be righteous in the sanctity of a radiant Heaven than the relatively brutish slums we call earth.

What does God really know about my struggles? What does God really know about what it's like to try to live a good life in a world that tempts us in endless ways to do otherwise?

In the Epistle to the Hebrews, the writer of this letter to the church in Jerusalem answers our objection, "For we do not have a high priest who is unable to empathize with our weaknesses, but we have one who has been tempted in every way, just as we are – yet he did not sin."[121]

Man-made religions have priests that act as go-betweens between God and people, and often they can seem as distant and unsympathetic to our plight as a God far off in Heaven. Yet the first Christians realized that their "high priest" was no longer an allegedly quasi-holy man, but a truly holy God.

How can God be for us an intermediary to Godself? In the incarnation, God became flesh and blood, being emptied of divine power and privilege.[122] In Jesus, God was not floating six inches off the ground merely appearing to be human. In Jesus, God experienced the fullness of what it means to be human, both the good and bad. Jesus formed deep friendships, held children in his arms, celebrated at weddings, talked late

---

[121] Hebrews 4:15
[122] John 1:14; Philippians 2:5-8

into the night at dinner parties, and saw the sun rise and set against the rugged backdrop of the Judean wilderness. He also witnessed first-hand all the effects of a world estranged from God – broken relationships, political and social injustice, natural corruption of the body with disease and the environment with famine, and death all around him. He responded with healing compassion, deep grief, and justified anger. [123] He endured hunger, poverty, exhaustion, social rejection, and hatred.

Experiencing all our fallen world had to throw at him, Jesus was tempted to sin. Jesus felt the existential anxiety to not trust God that our primordial parents felt, and the allure to give in to the choices of least resistance that offered gratification. Greed, rage, lust, pride – Jesus was tempted in all these ways, but he did not turn to them. [124] He chose trust and intimacy with his Heavenly Father above everything else.

This was not to shame us, as if God was calling our bluff about how hard it was to be human and wanted to prove that we had exaggerated the difficulty. God was not unsympathetically wagging a divine finger at us from Heaven. No, God lived among us to demonstrate that God was in complete solidarity with us. God's love was not pristine and orderly, but messy and willing to get down in the dirt and grime with us. In Jesus, the Son of Man, God chose to empathize with us fully. The incarnation proves that God is no stranger to our struggles and our temptations, but that God was willing to enter into *our* sin without committing sin.

As a result, Saint Paul calls Jesus "The New Adam," or new humanity. [125] Where we failed and continue to fail, Jesus resisted sin as the New Adam, providing humanity a new

---

[123] It is clear from the life Jesus led that anger at evil is not inherently sinful. Jesus insulted hypocritical religious elites and drove out the corrupt money-changers in the Temple who had taken over the area reserved for non-Jews to worship the God of Israel.

[124] Hebrews 4:15

[125] Romans 5:12-18; 1 Corinthians 15:45

trajectory to grow into. Now there could be a trajectory not of estrangement and death, but of relationship and life.

God Absorbs Our Sin

The early Christians struggled to make sense of the death of Jesus. Why did God die on a Roman cross? The dilemma, however, was impossible to avoid. All the gospels record Jesus declaring that his very mission was to die. It was no accident. The gospel accounts by Matthew and Luke even show Jesus, wavering on the eve of his arrest, asking his Heavenly Father to reconcile humanity by some other means if possible. [126] The Father's "no" to his Son's request to be spared meant that the death of Jesus was not one of many options God had for reconciling the world, but the only hope for reconciliation.

On the cross, Jesus sacrificed himself for the sin of the world. This became known as the *atonement*, the act that created harmony between God and humanity. What about the death of God though was necessary for the atonement for sin? Here too, early Christians offered a myriad of explanations. [127]

One pair of early ideas, known as the *ransom theory* and the *Christus victor theory*, said that God masterminded a plan to trick the Adversary and overcome the forces of evil. Satan was understood to have dominion over a fallen world's sinful inhabitants. We, by our own rejection of God, had given ourselves over to the one who opposed God, and so Satan held deceased souls in spiritual prison while awaiting our inevitable arrival. However, seeing an opportunity to kill the Son of God, the Adversary used the evil forces of this world to do his bidding. Through the cross, God sacrificially endured the

---

[126] Matthew 26:39; Luke 22:42

[127] At least seven in total, with some more obscure than others. For the sake of clarity, I present the five most historical atonement theories and group those most similar together in pairs.

assault of both spiritual and human evil for our sake. Jesus as the Son of Man was consumed in death, but Jesus as the Son of God broke into Satan's spiritual prison and demolished the walls from within. For anyone willing to walk out with him, Christ in his compassion was liberating the captives and leading them to freedom. In doing so, Jesus declared victory over the forces of evil, heralding their retreat and ultimate defeat by the Kingdom of God.

St. Augustine of Hippo in the fourth century, described it in a similar way, with an emphasis on bailing humanity out from debt that sinners had fallen into with Satan. He explains, "The Redeemer came and the deceiver was overcome. What did our Redeemer do to our Captor? In payment for us He set the trap, His Cross, with His blood for bait. He [Satan] could indeed shed that blood; but he deserved not to drink it. By shedding the blood of One who was not his debtor, he was forced to release his debtors." [128] Likewise, Irenaeus in the second century declared that on the cross, Christ was "both waging war against our enemy, and crushing him who had at the beginning led us away captives in Adam."[129]

If this all sounds a bit dramatic, you may be surprised that this only echoes the same language that Jesus himself used. Calling himself a "ransom for many," he described himself as a robber that would overpower the Adversary and rob him of his possessions – us![130]

The image that might summarize the ransom and Christus victor theories best could be a rescue mission from Satan's fortress, that not only rescues the captives but turns the tide of a cosmic war.

Another early theory that eventually reached completion by the sixteenth century in the Western Church,

---

[128] Augustine, Sermon 80, "On the New Testament," circa 400 CE
[129] Irenaeus, *Against Heresies*, Chapter 21, circa 180 CE
[130] Mark 10:45; Luke 11:20-22

known as *satisfaction theory*, emphasized the legal nature of the cross and that God (not Satan) was the true debtor of humanity. We sinful humans were guilty of sin that violated the dignity of our neighbor and even more so, of God.[131] Since God is perfectly just, God could not let the suffering and evil we created and participated in go unanswered. If God were to simply forgive us, with no consequences, God would be violating the integrity of God's own justice and consistency of God's perfect character. Nor could we hope to make sufficient restitution or amends for the wrongs we have done. Even if we could repay every person we ever hurt to their satisfaction, how could our finite lives earn forgiveness from an infinite and eternal God? Unable to provide our own restitution, God lovingly supplied God's own restitution for us on the cross. In this way, justice and mercy would embrace.[132] The perfect life of the Son of God was exchanged on our behalf, and so satisfied the justice of God, though it was the result of this very exchange that maintained God's mercy.

In the eleventh century, the theologian Anselm of Canterbury shared this joyous formula at the end of his masterwork, *Why the God-Man?*. He exulted, "The heavenly kingdom must be filled with men, and if this cannot happen unless the satisfaction is made for sin — satisfaction which no one can make but God, and no one ought to make but man — then it is necessary for the God-Man to make it."[133]

Just what was satisfied though? Some, like Anselm, have said it was a spiritual debt owed to God that our sin created, which could only be paid by a being of infinite virtue. Others, like the Protestant Reformer John Calvin in the sixteenth century, said it was also a punishment that our sin

---

[131] Psalm 57:4

[132] Psalm 85:10

[133] Saint Anselm, *Proslogium; Monologium; An Appendix in Behalf of the Fool by Gaunilon; and Cur Deus Homo*, (Chicago: Open Court, 1903).

deserved, which could only be meted out on one who was of infinite innocence and obedience. Both reflect on the images found in the Old Testament covenants, where animal sacrifices temporarily satisfied the stain of sin and the punishment for sin. Saint Paul, while he was under house-arrest, supplied the biblical rationale for satisfaction theory in his letter to the Colossians by writing, "God made [us] alive together with him, having forgiven us all our trespasses, by canceling the record of debt that stood against us with its legal demands. This he set aside, nailing it to the cross."[134]

The image that might sum up the satisfaction theory best is a courtroom where the judge (or jury) find you guilty beyond a shadow of a doubt, but the judge, motivated by jaw-dropping compassion, comes down from the bench to pay both your fine and serve your sentence.

The last major theory about the atonement is the *recapitulation theory,* which is most widely held among the Eastern Orthodox Church. In this view, sin is seen as something like a deadly virus that has infected all of humanity. Its effects are always terminal in three major ways: physically, socially, and especially spiritually. As history has clearly proven, we are incapable of curing ourselves from the ravages of sin and death. To save humanity from this death spiral, the cross becomes the point in human history where God enters into the disease of death, becoming the antidote that can reverse the course of the pandemic and heal humanity. Jesus Christ is understood as the New Adam in an expanded role, taking on the fullness of humanity to heal it fully. Christ's human death was therefore the means whereby death itself was treated, allowing humanity to be cured of its sin disease and spiritually uniting the community of humanity with the Triune God.

---

[134] Colossians 2:14

In the early fourth century, the theologian Athanasius of Alexandria, while penning the definitive doctrine of the incarnation, also crystalized this understanding of atonement that had been building since Irenaeus in the second century began speaking of a cosmic renewal. Athanasius concludes, "Thus of taking a body like our own, because all our bodies were liable to the corruption of death, He surrendered His body to death in place of all, and offered it to the Father. This He did for sheer love for us, so that in His death all might die, and the law of death thereby be abolished because, when He had fulfilled in His body that for which it was appointed, [death] was therefore voided of its power for men."[135]

Now united in Christ, whatever Christ overcomes, is overcome on our behalf. Whatever Christ restores, is restored on our behalf. Since Christ overcomes death and restores humanity to relationship with God, we once again have access to eternal life and divine intimacy. There are too many Scriptures from which the recapitulation theory is drawn from to mention here, but perhaps the most succinct is given by Saint Paul in his letter to the Corinthian church. He assured us, "For as by a human came death, by a human has come also the resurrection of the dead. For as in Adam all die, so also in Christ shall all be made alive."[136]

The image that might sum up the recapitulation theory best is a hospital where the doctor provides a life-saving cure from the veins of his own donated blood.

There has been an unfortunate temptation throughout Christian history to overemphasize a single atonement theory to the point of oversimplifying God's character and motivations. However, it seems undeniable that all of these understandings of the atonement are all consistent within the framework of wider Christian and Jewish theology, draw from

---

[135] Athanasius, *On the Incarnation*, circa 313 CE.
[136] 1 Corinthians 15:21-22

the authoritative well of Scripture, and paint inspiring metaphors of what God did on the cross. It is best to believe all of them, to some extent, as complementary concepts rather than competitive doctrines.

All historic atonement theories have a consistent feature that Christians define as *substitutionary*, that is, Jesus Christ substituted himself in our place to achieve what we never could accomplish on our own.[137] Saint Paul declared that we can be reconciled to God because "for our sake he made him to be sin who knew no sin, so that in him we might become the righteousness of God."[138] This exchange is multi-faceted and completely sufficient. Whether it is victory over evil, satisfying the justice of God for my sin, or healing me from sin's cancerous grip, Jesus made atonement in my place so that I could be redeemed from my estrangement and brought back to God. The moment I trust this, I experience what Christians call *justification* before God. This is not only forgiveness for my sins, but an embrace of who I am. With this love from Heaven, my relationship with God has been reconciled through the cross.

God Defeats Our Sin

If the cross had been the end of Christ's work, however, the Early Church would not have spent hundreds of years reflecting on its power. Indeed, there would be no Church at all. The atoning death of Jesus only has power because of the resurrection, and the resurrection only has meaning because of his atoning death. There cannot be one without the other.

---

[137] Some Christians believe a "substitutionary" dynamic only applies to the satisfaction theory. This seems to unnecessarily acquiesce to 16th century Reformation categories, and misses the wider and historical nature of substitution as it relates to our own failed efforts to reconcile with God.
[138] 2 Corinthians 5:21

The resurrection of Christ vindicated the claims of Christ. There were other men in Jewish history who claimed to be the Messiah, the savior of the Hebrew people. They too met death at the hands of their enemies, but they all remained dead. The resurrection of Jesus of Nazareth was proof that he was not just the Son of Man, but also the Son of God.

The resurrection though is not simply the grand finale in a series of miracles meant to prove Jesus' divinity. Jesus does not dance through the tomb's opening while shouting, "Ta-da!" to the bewildered disciples. The resurrection is so much more. In the resurrection of Jesus, we witness the Triune God's guarantee that the effects of humanity's estrangement are now being reversed.

The first consequence of our estrangement was a broken relationship between humanity and God, and subsequently discord within our own minds and with one another. We are inherently relational beings who are more than capable of fraying the strongest bonds through our apathy and selfishness.

Despite his murder by his enemies and abandonment by his friends, the resurrected Christ did not exact revenge on his killers or berate his faithless disciples, but instead offered forgiveness to all. In John's gospel account, Jesus even specifically seeks out Peter, the disciple who publicly denied Jesus three times. Three times he asks Peter if he loves him, revealing an emotional encounter that restores not only their relationship, but also restores Peter's role as leader of the ragtag band of disciples. Jesus tells the disciples that the future followers of Christ will be known by their love for one another.[139]

Jesus' post-resurrection restoration of his disciples speaks to another essential Christian belief that while God

---

[139] John 21:15-17; 13:35

accepts us just as we are, God never leaves us as we are.[140] Once God justifies the person who trusts in the atoning work of Christ, in a gradual process known as *sanctification,* we enter into what is a lifelong journey of turning away from sin and conforming our lives to the love of God. The resurrection guarantees that for whomever is in Christ, the Holy Spirit is sanctifying that person by empowering them to defeat their own sin, heal their psychological wounds, and restore their relationships with others.

The second consequence of our estrangement was injustice to our neighbor. The powerful oppressed the weak. The wealthy took advantage of the poor. Hate and envy are inevitably aimed back towards the elite. Sexism, racism, classism, nationalism, and heterosexism seem nearly timeless now, seared into the sociology of cultures.

Yet Jesus, in his arrest and execution, was himself the victim of an overlapping series of injustices. There was no person in human history more innocent than Jesus, yet he was put to death by the most enlightened legal system of his day. The evil powers of this world, both human and demonic, did their worst to the Son of God. In the resurrection though, God emerged victorious over those powers and as Saint Paul's letter to the Colossians declared, "disarmed the rulers and authorities and put them to open shame, by triumphing over them in him."[141] The resurrection guarantees that injustice will not carry on forever, and that God will hold the forces of evil to account.

The third consequence of our estrangement was the corruption of our earth. The planet seems doomed by entropy. We destroy the environment even as the environment seems to exact revenge on us. In the last 500 years, humans have wiped out 322 animal species and have seen upwards of 20,000

---

[140] Titus 2:14; Colossians 3:5-14
[141] Colossians 2:15

species risk extinction. [142] Climate change, regardless of whether one considers it a natural phenomenon or driven almost unilaterally by civilization's carbon emissions, threatens to cause as much death and human dislocation as a world war.

Fortunately for the environment, Jesus not only demonstrated his power over the natural world by calming a destructive storm, but the physical nature of the resurrection points to the truth that God is committed to creation. [143] Had Jesus returned to life in spiritual angelic-like form, we could surmise that the physical things of this earth are only passing away to a more important spiritual realm. If so, why care for ecosystems and species in the meantime? The physical resurrection of Jesus in a glorified body shows that the natural world is not meant to pass into a spiritual world. Even during his ascension into Heaven, Jesus did not shed his physical body. The natural world – this visible material creation of God – will be renewed by God to its fullest beauty.

Saint Paul explicitly anticipates this, teaching the first Christians in Rome, "For the creation was subjected to futility, not willingly, but because of him who subjected it, in hope that the creation itself will be set free from its bondage to corruption and obtain the freedom of the glory of the children of God. For we know that the whole of creation has been groaning together in the pains of childbirth until now." [144] God made this planet as an expression of God's creative love, and God will not abandon it.

The fourth consequence of our estrangement was death to ourselves. Scripture calls this "the last enemy." [145] It is the enemy that leads a grievous parade of loved ones to the

---

[142] Dirzo, R., H. S. Young, M. Galetti, G. Ceballos, N. J. B. Isaac, and B. Collen. "Defaunation in the Anthropocene." *Science* 345, no. 6195 (2014): 401–6.

[143] Mark 4:35-41

[144] Romans 8:20-22

[145] 1 Corinthians 15:26

grave, the slow decay and eventual death of our own physical bodies, and the evaporation of our spirits unto some unknown afterlife – or perhaps oblivion. Even our universe is currently destined to die in coldness and isolation, expressing our own fate of estrangement writ large on a cosmic scale.

Death may be the last enemy scheduled for defeat, but it was likely the first realization for the disciples of Jesus. Christ overcame death itself. This was not just a temporary resuscitation from death as with some of the people Jesus raised from the dead during his ministry, but a return to life that which was indisputably permanent and enduring. For the first time in human history, death suffered an irreversible defeat. Jesus came into the world proclaiming the Kingdom of God, but now he also proclaims, "I am the Living One; I was dead, and now look, I am alive for ever and ever! And I hold the keys of death and Hades."[146] Since the beginning of history, life has been unable to resist being defined by death. Now, with the demise of death as a real possibility, nothing could be more revolutionary in its consequences.

In addition, Saint Paul in a letter to the Colossian church, points out that Christ is only "the beginning, the firstborn from the dead, that in everything he might be preeminent."[147] We too are promised a resurrection like that of Jesus. Time will not be the acid that erodes all things. In Christ, time is the refining fire that reveals the glory of that which is imperishable. The estrangement that leads to death will not be the final word. For those in Christ, Christ is the final and only Word. [148] And Christ's pronouncement is this: "I am the resurrection and the life. Whoever believes in me, though he die, yet shall he live."[149]

---

[146] Revelation 1:18
[147] Colossians 1:18
[148] In reference to John 1:1, many early Christians actually referred to Jesus simply as "The Word."
[149] John 11:25

So What? Trusting in the Love from Heaven

One of the greatest problems – if not the greatest problem – people have with believing in the God of the Bible is the disconnect that they feel between a God who claims to be loving and a world so full of hate. Philosophers call this the question of *theodicy*. In a globalized society, we are perhaps overwhelmed more than ever with the extent of suffering and evil around us. Many of us have experienced tragedy personally.

The question of the thoughtful skeptic thus arises. Suggested first by the fourth century BCE Greek philosopher Epicurus and later weaponized by Enlightenment philosopher David Hume, he quipped, "Is God willing to prevent evil, but not able? Then he is not omnipotent. Is he able, but not willing? Then he is malevolent. Is he both able and willing? Then whence cometh evil? Is he neither able nor willing? Then why call him God?"[150]

There is certainly no singular response to this question. Cruder forms of Christianity have offered vague assurances of a divine plan that will benefit you if you resist the temptation to doubt and conjure up enough faith. More stoic Christians have offered that God, as wholly "other" and outside of our fallen and finite conceptions, cannot be accurately judged with metrics of "good" or "evil." Even recently, some progressive Christians have said that God is not as omnipotent as we've imagined God to be, and that God is gradually working with us to eliminate suffering and evil.

Regardless, the philosopher's dilemma is not the same as the average person's dilemma. A good philosopher or theologian can resolve the tension of suffering and evil with a loving God through a few lofty formulas or rhetorical spins.

---

[150] Hume, David. *Dialogues Concerning Natural Religion: By David Hume, Esq.* (London?: 1779).

This may logically help us wrestle with the reality of genocide or terrorism, terrible but usually distant evils for most modern people living in the Western World, and yet these same formulas are often cold comfort when tragedy hits home. When cancer strikes a loved one. When a car crash ends the life of young person. When the wealthy and powerful people we see in the news create injustice with seeming impunity – and then get re-elected or promoted. The despair we feel is more real than a formula. The rage we feel cannot be assuaged with a spiritual cliché. We want to know if all this suffering and evil negates our waning hope that God really loves us.

It is the very life, death, and resurrection of Jesus that provides an assurance to us greater than calculated philosophical arguments or syrupy, spiritual clichés. In the incarnation of God, we witness the almighty God of the universe willingly take on all our human weaknesses. We may not receive an answer for our suffering, but we know God loves us enough to voluntarily suffer with us. Jesus wept with people and for people. This alone – the solidarity of God with wretched humanity – could suffice as proof of God's love for God's creation.

Still, for those of us who have experienced great suffering, the anger may not subside. Our indignation burns white hot. Sometimes at life's dice rolling us snake-eyes with disease and misfortune. Sometimes at our oppressors and betrayers who have inflicted so much pain upon us. Sometimes our wrath is even aimed directly towards God, who in some way we know bears responsibility for allowing all this suffering and evil to exist in the first place. Yet in those very moments that we hate God, and perhaps wonder if we are hating anything more than a figment of our imagination, those moments are speaking back to the cross as much as the cross is speaking forward to us.

On the cross, Christ did not just endure the wages of sin or pay the spiritual debt God deserved from us. On the cross, Christ did not just endure the assault of evil forces or vicariously take on the wrath of God. On the cross, *I myself* lashed out with the anger I thought God deserved as payback for the mismanagement of the world. *I myself* unleashed wrath upon God for what I thought were inexcusable failures to protect me and those I loved. Despite all of that rage, God replied to me as he did to Judas, "My friend, do what you feel like you need to do."[151] God did not just die for you out of love. Out of love, God allowed you to be the self-righteous executioner.

This still does not blithely explain away suffering or evil. God is not interested in providing clichés or formulas. God answers our suffering by entering into our suffering, and allowing us to make God suffer. God answers evil by speaking truth to its face, and allowing us to spit in the face of God.

The love from Heaven to humanity, from God to you, can be trusted because the incarnation and atonement is at every step and every dimension a declaration of love. God's love from Heaven is strong. It is at least as strong as my own doubt. Even in my darkest nights, my trust can lean not on the strength of my own confidence, but on the strength of the one who has already seen me at my worst and lowest, and weeps with me.[152]

A Beautiful Identity

Who are you? Yes. That question again.

What are we to do with it? Don't think you can escape the question. The rest of humanity that has gone before us has had no such success.

---

[151] Matthew 26:50
[152] John 11:35

There is also no shortage of identities you can select. Religions, philosophies, ethics, and political ideologies are all peddling potential choices. Some have even tried to synthesize a pseudo-Christian identity with their own.

The Triune God, though, will have none of that. Why? Because the identity that God won for you was achieved at far too great a price to be split up among that which is immeasurably less precious. What's more, this transcendent identity is far better than the offerings of any human-created religion or ideology.

Where does this identity originate? Saint Paul saw our identity forged in the death and resurrection of Jesus Christ. Paul wrote to the church in Rome that, "We were buried therefore with him by baptism into death, in order that, just as Christ was raised from the dead by the glory of the Father, we too might walk in newness of life."[153]

In this verse we can see our identity begins with our association to something other than ourselves. This would not be unusual from many other identities, except nearly all identities associate us with a human leader, organization, or cause. The foundation of Christian identity is not built on any human institution, not even the Church. Christian identity is built on associating with the work and person of Christ.

The first followers of Jesus Christ called themselves followers of "The Way," but eventually picked up the moniker "Christian" from the pagans around them. Far from a term of endearment, it was probably used in derision. In the pagans' view, these early followers of The Way seemed so single-minded about becoming "Little Christs" that Christian seemed like a fitting label to slap on them. The followers of The Way, however, didn't seem to mind the name change. What was meant as an insult, was in fact, a badge of honor.[154]

---

[153] Romans 6:4
[154] Acts 5:41

Other than association with Christ through his death and resurrection, what does this identity grant us? Saint Paul continues teaching the first Roman Christians, explaining, "For you did not receive the spirit of slavery to fall back into fear, but you have received the Spirit of adoption as sons, by whom we cry, 'Abba! Father!' The Spirit himself bears witness with our spirit that we are children of God, and if children, then heirs — heirs of God and fellow heirs with Christ, if indeed we suffer with him in order that we may also be glorified with him."[155]

Our identity with Christ bestows on us a status greater than all others. In Christ, God has adopted us.[156] This may come as a surprise to some. There is a popular myth that somewhere in the Bible there is a passage about all people being "God's children," yet the Christian faith has taught the opposite. The Scriptures tell us that because of The Fall, we are born into the world as spiritual orphans.[157] Our natural state as orphans is simply another consistent metaphor for our estrangement from God.

To take on an identity in Christ provides us then with another picture of our reconciliation, this time in the form of adoption. God has sought us out from a great distance and even greater cost, adopted us as his very own spiritual children, and made us co-heirs with everything Christ earned. Where God was once a distant deity, now we can call God not just Father in the abstract, but the Aramaic word *Abba*, that is, "*My* Father." As a child of God, my status is that of extravagant access by the grace of God and intimacy with the will of God.

To have an identity gifted to us by Christ also provides us with answers to the two existential questions every person

---

[155] Romans 8:15-17
[156] John 1:11-13
[157] Ephesians 2:3

wrestles to answer, what is my true worth and who is my truest self?

First, we know our true worth as Christians. I am a dearly loved and adopted child of God. My value has been certified by God. No one else in the world has any right to say I am anything less, or offer a deal to somehow make me greater. Even on days where I fail to act like a child of God, or when I do not believe I truly am a child of God, my status is not forfeited. God has adopted us. My rebelliousness on any given day will never convince my heavenly parent to make me an orphan again. Therefore, my identity is secured on God's faithfulness as a perfect, merciful, and generous Father – always running to meet me when I am ready to return home.[158]

Second, we know our truest selves as Christians. Our identity is not ultimately found in our heritage, sexual orientation, ethnicity, sex, gender, or nationality. Regardless of whether those markers are for us a source of either shame or pride, a source of oppression or privilege – we transcend them in Christ. How did the first Christians understand this?

The citizens of the Roman Empire would customarily declare in an oath, "Caesar is Lord," as a litmus test for loyalty. Risking their lives, Christians instead proclaimed, "Jesus is Lord." Since they followed a resurrected Messiah, they knew the Kingdom of God was greater and more glorious than the Empire of Rome. Whether they were a privileged Roman citizen or a peasant living in a far-flung occupied province, each Christian believed themselves to be citizens of a greater country. While still law-abiding, Christians understood their relationship to the state would be held loosely because their true "citizenship [was] in Heaven."[159]

There was an ancient prayer recited by Jewish men that said, "Blessed are you O God, King of the Universe, who has

---

[158] Romans 8:16, 31-39; Luke 15:18-20
[159] Philippians 3:20

not made me a gentile [non-Jew], slave, or woman." Scandalously, the Book of Acts devotes its entire sixteenth chapter to recording that when a church began in the Greco-Roman city of Philippi, the first three converts of their Jewish pastor were none other than a gentile, a slave, and a woman. That pastor was Saint Paul, who would later write, "There is no longer Jew or Gentile, slave or free, male and female. For you are all one in Christ Jesus."[160]

Eunuchs, an ancient term for men who were seen as outside the heterosexual spectrum,[161] were forbidden by Jewish law from participating in temple worship. Despite a clear biblical injunction against the inclusion of this sexual minority,[162] the Apostle Philip's first convert was an African eunuch. The eunuch then immediately asked Philip, "What is there that can stand in the way of my being baptized?"[163] With this new identity in Christ, Philip provocatively made no objection nor listed any provisos. According to Church tradition, that eunuch became the first Christian missionary to Ethiopia.

Family and tribal ties in Jesus' time were designed to protect scarce financial resources and vital social status, but Jesus directly created a more inclusive definition of family. "Whoever does the will of God is my brother, sister, and mother," he declared.[164] The first Christians not only endured the humiliation of being disowned by some of their pagan families, but also became known throughout the Roman Empire for adopting orphans. They realized that because of their adoption in Christ, then not even familial blood ties could command greater loyalty than the Triune God.

---

[160] Galatians 3:28
[161] Matthew 19:12
[162] Deuteronomy 23:1-3; Leviticus 21:18-20
[163] Acts 8:36
[164] Mark 3:35

This clarity demonstrated by the early Christians allows me to see through the shifting and often self-serving systems that vie for my allegiance today, just as it empowers me to see past the limitations those same systems of oppression and control try to place on me. I know *who* I am because of *whose* I am.

Still, my other identities and loyalties are not flattened into a homogeneous and dull "Christian identity," as if they no longer possess any worth. We do not divorce ourselves from our families or renounce our citizenship. We do not naively attempt to be apolitical, genderless, asexual, or colorblind. These backgrounds and experiences are formative to our sense of being and our relationship to the world around us, and the nature of a Three-in-One God is intrinsically capable of handling the complexity of our formative identities, vocations, and roles throughout the course of our lives. The Spirit heals those parts of us which are wounded, humbles those parts which are overbearing, and transforms those parts which are good for an even greater good.

Howard Thurman, one of the most influential theologians of the twentieth century, was born in 1899. His father died shortly after and his mother took on a domestic service job, relegating care of Thurman to his grandmother. A former slave and still illiterate, she was a woman who possessed an inner and outer strength that deeply imprinted upon Thurman. Where did she find this strength? It was a simple belief, but one that would undergird Thurman's brilliant intellect for years to come. His grandmother believed she was a child of God. She learned this at secret church meetings led by fellow slaves on the plantation. It was a belief so ingrained in her very being that it allowed her to talk to God even as her slave master tried to quote the Bible to dehumanize her and keep her subservient.

She knew better, and so Howard Thurman knew better too, despite the brutality of living in the Jim Crow American South which denied his humanity and disparaged his racial and ethnic identity as a Black American. Refusing to be victimized by such an oppressive culture, Howard pursued an advanced education, becoming a minister and theologian who taught at Howard University and Boston University. His work would form the theological core of the African-American Civil Rights movement and become a key teaching component of non-violent resistance for an entire generation. Martin Luther King Jr. was said to have carried a copy of Thurman's small but seminal work, *Jesus and the Disinherited*, in his pocket.

Some Christians have credited Thurman, both as a compliment and as an accusation, with developing a theology more political than spiritual. Yet, it was merely his grandmother's simple identity as an image-bearer of Christ extrapolated into seeking justice for racial oppression in America. Howard wrote in that little book carried by King, "The awareness of being a child of God tends to stabilize the ego and results in new courage, fearlessness, and power. I have seen it happen again and again."[165]

It is almost unfathomable, perhaps even absurd, to our secular age, that a person's identity would not be formed by the approval they might garner in the world's eyes – not by wealth, career, power, success, or attractiveness. It seems almost superhuman that my identity could resist manipulation by the descriptors the world attaches to me from birth – not heritage, sexual orientation, ethnicity, sex, gender, or nationality. This power, however, truly emanates from our heavenly adoption. Newly framed, these things can no longer be curses or entitlements, but rather redemptive blessings.

---

[165] Thurman, Howard. *Jesus and the Disinherited*. (New York: Abingdon-Cokesbury Press, 1949).

The revolutionary act of taking on Christ as my core and supreme identity is that I am no longer beholden to the expectations and prejudices of the world. Those expectations and prejudices set against me were nailed to the cross. Their authority over me has been nullified, their power displaced. Clothed in Christ with my baptism, I have been liberated from the gaze of the fallen world that seeks to shame me or gain power over me.[166] Eating and drinking the spiritual body and blood of Christ in the Eucharist, all the worldly towers of status, power, and privilege are leveled.[167]

As a child of God, adopted by a divine love that reached down to me and brought me home to a new family, I am now free to live into the fullness of the beautiful person I was created to be.

---

[166] Galatians 3:27
[167] 1 Corinthians 11:17-29

CHAPTER SIX
Hope In The Future

Many religious people hope that sometime in the future, after their deaths, an ethereal afterlife called *Heaven* exists. Yet the Christian faith's hope for the future is so much more than this. This hope fundamentally rests in what is known as the *Second Coming*, when Christ will return to earth.

This arrival, however, will be quite unlike his first. In the first, Christ came in weakness. In the second, Christ will come in power. In the first, Christ came in obscurity. In the second, Christ will come in glory. In the first, Christ came in mercy and grace. In the second, Christ will come in judgment and justice.[168]

The Bible describes the Second Coming using language that is assuring and intimidating, joyous and terrifying. We

---

[168] Mark 13:26; Jude 1:14-15; Rev. 22:12-13

might imagine it would be exciting to meet God, but the consistent narrative of the Bible shows that you would be more likely to pass out from terror or run away screaming for fear of death. In case there was any ambiguity about the divine wrath of Jesus from the gospels, since he mercifully left no body count in his first appearance, the end of the Bible clears up any misconceptions. The Prince of Peace wields a metaphorical sword.[169] With this sword, God will not only cut down all lies with truth, but it will also cut down the last stubborn bastions of evil and oppression with total destruction.

It all sounds a bit fantastic, right? On the other hand, what apocalyptic scenario wouldn't be dramatic? Certainly not any worth great anticipation. If the world as we know it is going to end, we should expect it to stretch the boundaries of our imagination at least a little bit. Still, why do Christians believe this particular destiny of the world? Primarily, because Jesus himself is recorded fifteen times in the gospel accounts teaching that he would return.[170] If we become convinced that Jesus is the incarnate Son of God who defeated death itself, it's reasonable to believe Jesus when he says he'll be back. Additionally, Christians rely on the implications of God's character to hope there will be a once-and-for-all reversal of the effects of sin and estrangement. Our rebellion against God could only end in either God destroying humanity or God reconciling humanity, and since we know God desires the latter, we trust that God will reconcile the world fully. Given the brokenness of the world, reconciliation of that magnitude would certainly be fantastic.

This "study of last things" is called *eschatology*, and much of what the Christian faith believes about a Christ-focused eschatology comes from Saint Paul's letters and from

---

[169] Revelation 19:15
[170] For example, Mark 8:38, Matt. 24:30-31, Luke 12:40, and John 14:3.

the Book of Revelation. [171] Conversely, a widespread belief among the early Christians about the return of Christ existed well before the Book of Revelation was written around 96 CE. One of the earliest creedal statements for Christians, developed only a few years after Christ's death and resurrection, was spoken every Sunday while celebrating communion and finished with, "For as often as you eat this bread and drink the cup, you proclaim the Lord's death until he *comes*." Old Testament prophecies about God healing the world also informed a holistic expectation about what the end of this world and the beginning of the next would be like.[172]

At different periods in history, individual Christians have tried to interpret, with great specificity, the meaning of the events of Revelation and applied them to people and events in their own time. These interpretations usually turn out embarrassing in retrospect. In reality, the Christian tradition has never been uniform on how to interpret Revelation, and typically divides along four views.

The first view, preterism, is that Revelation cryptically describes a short timeline pertaining to the ancient Roman empire and the destruction of Jerusalem. The second, historicism, describes specific events played out over thousands of years, often related to corruption in Roman Catholicism. The third, futurism, describes events mostly in a distant future at the end of the age, often with literal dragons and beasts or with modern military technology. The fourth, idealism, understands this final book of the Bible as a repeating allegory applicable to every generation of Christians. The closest scholarly consensus among historic Christian denominations tends to embrace a mix of preterist and idealist interpretations.

---

[171] And for some Christian traditions, the gospel accounts themselves are even more influential than the Book of Revelation.

[172] As one of many examples, compare Isaiah 63:1-6 and Joel 3:13 to Revelations 14:14-20.

Suffice to say, Revelation is an altogether one of the most complicated, wondrous, and confusing books in the Bible. Should you be daring enough to read Revelation,[173] it is probably best to read it as a pastoral letter of spiritual encouragement to first-century Christians struggling with growing persecution as well as a prophetic commentary that foreshadows the final victory of God over all evil.

The End of Sin and a New Earth

Regardless of how different Christian traditions interpret Revelation and the end of this age, there is agreement that when God returns to Earth, it will be the end of sin.

The end of sin will mean that a broken world has finally been made whole again. The effects of our sin and estrangement from God wrought relational brokenness, injustice in society, corruption of creation, and death to all life. The Christian faith has hope in a future where those four effects will be undone, where all things will be reconciled to Christ. [174] With our estrangement from God finally over, the world will look quite differently than it does now. The old world will have "passed away," but this new world will not be a brand new planet.[175] After all, God created this planet, and what God creates God cares about.

Perhaps more surprising is that this same world will be radically renewed, but not restarted. Though the Tree of Life is symbolically replanted for the healing of all peoples,[176] this will not be a reboot of humanity to some primordial Eden. Christ has already come as the "New Adam" and moved the arc of redemption forward. The story that God started in a garden

---

[173] Eastern Orthodoxy, for example, does not typically recommend it. In their view, it's too weird.
[174] Colossians 1:19-20; Revelation 21:1-4
[175] Revelation 21:1
[176] Revelation 22:2

will be completed in a city. [177] Art and architecture will remain. [178] Commerce and technology will remain. [179] Our work in fields like these matter – even the work you are doing right now – because what is truly good and just has the potential to be carried by God into eternity. What is not good and just either will be removed or repaired. Not just bad art and ugly architecture, but everything we know that has been deformed by sin will be purified like dross from gold.

There will be no more degradation of our ecosystems, and there will be harmony between humanity and nature like never before, and all diseases will be cured.

There will be no more war. Our fighter jets will be scrapped to build farm tractors and rockets for exploring the vast reaches of space. [180]

There will be no more poverty. Capitalism will be rendered obsolete and communism unnecessary, and the individual choices that put people in poverty will not be desirable options.

There will be no more injustice. Political tyranny will give way to God's perfect rule; racism will give way to a celebration of all ethnicities, and the discriminatory "-isms" based on human differences will give way to complete equality and a submission to the truth that all people are made in the precious image of God.

There will finally be no more estrangement. Relationships between God, people, and within ourselves will be at last reconciled.

This final piece of reconciliation might strike you as the least wondrous. How could there *not* be relational

---

[177] Revelation 21:2
[178] Revelation 21:12-21
[179] Revelation 21:24
[180] This specific detail is, of course, speculative. It is inspired from the prophecy in Isaiah 2:4, "and they shall beat their swords into plowshares, and their spears into pruning hooks; nation shall not lift up sword against nation, neither shall they learn war anymore."

reconciliation when God takes over the world? However, this implies something which often shocks people. First, it means we will still remember people in the new earth from the old earth. We will remember our family and spouses, but also our rivals and enemies. Nearly everything – perhaps everything – of our memories will be retained. There is no indication in the Bible that God will do a "mind wipe" on us.

Still, if our minds themselves will be reconciled perfectly, with no more shame and "every tear wiped from our eyes,"[181] how will we not still be haunted by the past? How will we not grieve over the people we cared about who we do not find in the new earth? Aren't there certain people, who either because we love *or* hate now in this life, that their absence *or* presence in Heaven would make our happiness impossible?

In that mid-twentieth-century fantasy novel about the division between Heaven and hell called *The Great Divorce*, C.S. Lewis depicts an encounter between a wife who has been in Heaven inviting her deceased husband, who has until now been languishing in hell, to join her in Heaven. Surprisingly, he refuses, demanding to first hear from her how miserable she was without him.

> "'Look here,' said the husband. 'We've got to face this.' He was using his 'manly' bullying tone this time: the one for bringing women to their senses.
>
> 'Darling,' said the Lady to the man, 'there's nothing to face. You don't want me to have been miserable for misery's sake. You only think I must have been if I loved you. But if you'll only wait you'll see that isn't so.'

---

[181] Revelation 21:4

'Love!' said the husband striking his forehead with his hand: then, a few notes deeper, 'Love! Do you know the meaning of the word?'

'How should I not?' said the Lady. 'I am in love. In love, do you understand? Yes, now I love truly.'

'You mean,' said the man, 'you mean -you did not love me truly in the old days?'

'Only in a poor sort of way,' she answered. 'I have asked you to forgive me. There was a little real love in it. But what we called love down there was mostly the craving to be loved. In the main I loved you for my own sake: because I needed you.'

'And now!' said the man with a hackneyed gesture of despair. 'Now, you need me no more?'

'But of course not!' said the Lady; and her smile made me wonder how both the phantoms could refrain from crying out with joy. 'What needs could I have,' she said, 'now that I have all? I am full now, not empty. I am in Love Himself, not lonely. Strong, not weak. You shall be the same. Come and see. We shall have no need for one another now: we can begin to love truly.'"

Lewis's tale derives itself from his faith about the power of God's love for those who enter into it. The love of God is so complete that it will allow us to notice missing relationships without feeling we have been deprived. It will be so restorative it will allow us to look back on the mistakes of our first life and feel no shame.[182]

Reconciliation from our estrangement to God, with one another, and within ourselves will mean that we will not just be loved, but held *within* love.[183] This kind of love will make what currently seems impossible, finally possible.

---

[182] Isaiah 54:4
[183] 1 John 3:1

The Resurrection of the Dead

You may have noticed there is one consequence of sin that has been left conspicuously absent from how the world will be different when Christ returns – death. Though death is no doubt intimidating, you may think I am giving it more than its proper due here. This is primarily for the sake of clarity, since the undoing of death is one of the most misunderstood beliefs of the Christian faith.

Nearly as many Christians as non-Christians would say that the Christian hope for the future involves leaving our mortal bodies to worldly decay and having our immortal souls sent up to heavenly bliss. If this is how you understood the Christian afterlife to work out, you would be in the majority. You would also be completely wrong. In fact, the Christian understanding of the afterlife is more the inverse of that adaptation.

All the authors of the New Testament, whose writings were illuminated by the light of the resurrected Christ, understood that death would not truly be defeated if every person who had ever died remained bones and ashes. Jewish theology, of which nearly all the New Testament writers came from, held that whatever God created was precious. Humans, who were made in the image of God and who could worship God, were certainly the most precious by this measure. Therefore, we find explicit references to the resurrection of the dead in the Hebrew books of Daniel and Isaiah, and in rabbinic commentary on how God would resurrect people throughout Jewish history.[184]

The Christian hope for the future embraced the same expectation of resurrection by God, especially since Jesus himself was resurrected. The first Christians were eyewitnesses to what the undoing of death could look like.

---

[184] Isaiah 26:19; Daniel 12:2

Saint Paul taught that our hope of an afterlife has two stages. First, upon our deaths we will immediately enter into the joyous presence of God and the other-dimensional place of Heaven. Paul says, "to be absent of the body is to be present with Christ,"[185] while Jesus in the gospel of Luke told a rebel who was about to die next to him that, "today you will be with me in paradise." [186] This notion of Heaven is what most Christians tend to imagine as their final destination, but Jesus, Saint Paul, and the final apocalyptic book of the Bible, Revelation, tell us this is only half of the story.

Since God intends to renew and reign over earth, the second stage reunites our souls with our bodies back on earth. At Christ's return, our corpses, regardless of their condition, will be restored to life. All those reconciled to God will no longer be in Heaven, but living again on earth in resurrected bodies. We will be restored not just to our previous condition when we were alive, but to what the Bible refers to as a new "glorified" state. Saint Paul writes, "So is it with the resurrection of the dead. What is sown is perishable; what is raised is imperishable. It is sown in dishonor; it is raised in glory. It is sown in weakness; it is raised in power."[187] In other words, these resurrected bodies will be recognizable as our own bodies, but without the imperfections and limitations the effects of sin previously imposed upon us.

I realize this notion of our carbon whirling back into new bodies may be alarming. This is understandable, since many of us in the West have a difficult psychological relationship to our bodies. So simply consider this: whatever you fear about this glorified body will not be realized, and whatever you fantasize about this resurrection will probably not turn out exactly as you imagined. We can rest assured that

---

[185] 2 Corinthians 5:8
[186] Luke 23:43
[187] 1 Corinthians 15:42-43

whatever happens, it will be part of God's plan for the best possible afterlife.

The Christian faith's hope for the future then is ultimately not being taken up to Heaven, but to witness Heaven being brought to earth. The eternal nature of Heaven will reverse the decay of earth. Our resurrected bodies will become proclamations that death has finally been undone.

Heaven, Hell, and Who Goes Where

"Go to hell!" is one of the harsher insults in Western culture, and for good reason.

If Heaven has been parodied as a disembodied paradise in the clouds, hell has been made out to be a burning torture pit with grotesque demons brandishing pitchforks and cauldrons for boiling departed humans. In most of our imaginations, whether Christian or not, it is some place between the devilishly comical and utterly horrifying.

There tends to be two unhelpful ways of talking about hell. On one hand, there are some conservative religious people who play up hell as a means of controlling people by fear. You must become a Christian, or go to the terrible hell that awaits your non-believing soul. You must fall in line with particular doctrines or rules of conduct – often something to do with sex – or be punished for all eternity with flames for your heretical or immoral ways.

This way of talking about hell has actually very limited Scriptural merit. Besides, most of the imagery we have of hell emerges not from the Bible, but from European Medieval and Renaissance art and literature. When we study the Bible, we discover mixed and even contradictory images of hell, meaning that these descriptions were never meant to be taken literally.[188]

Perhaps most importantly, this way of describing hell is simply incongruous with the nature of the heart of the Christian faith. If God desires relationship with us, a loving and healthy relationship cannot be motivated by fear or threat of punishment. At best, a punishment-based relationship reflects the nature of a distant government to its citizens, and while God is unmistakably described as king and judge, God is also described as friend, lover, father and even mother.[189] At worst though, this fear-based understanding of Christianity reflects the dynamic of an abuser. It is incompatible with everything else the Christian faith has come to trust about God's character.

Faced with a description of hell that creates an abusive God, the pendulum has also swung the other way. Some progressive religious people have said that if God is a God of love, perhaps we can just dispense with hell altogether? Certainly a loving God would never send people to a torture pit for an intellectual mistake of failing to believe that a first-century rabbi was divine. Certainly a loving God would never eternally condemn the billions of people who, through no fault of their own, lived and died in places that never permitted them to hear the gospel. Certainly a loving God would never consign to unquenchable fire those who have otherwise lived a morally upstanding life, full of acts of charity and kindness, while at the same time rewarding with Heaven relatively "bad" people who happened to believe in Christ as their spiritual golden ticket. How can the heart of the Christian faith possibly tolerate a doctrine like hell, much less want such a doctrine?

---

[188] Matthew 8:12, 22:13, and 25:30 describe hell as an outer darkness, while Revelation 21:8 describes it as a lake of fire and sulfur.

[189] Psalm 47:7; John 15:15; Song of Sol.; Ephesians 5:25; 1 Corinthians 8:6; Hosea 11:3-4; Isaiah 66:13

However, if we believe the Bible is our central and supreme source for revealing the true and surprising character of God, it is nearly impossible to negate the consistent biblical narrative of a future event of divine justice. There will be an alternative for people other than Heaven. In fact, Jesus talks more about hell than any other person in the Bible.[190] The duality of Heaven and hell appears unavoidable to the faithful Christian, but for the compassionate person, it also feels equally unfair.

The reason why Heaven and hell doesn't make sense to most thoughtful people is because Christians have often talked about them as a system of reward for "good" people – whatever that means to you – and punishment for "bad" people – whatever that also means to you. There are plenty of passages in Scripture that mention reward and punishment,[191] yet this is not the only way that Jesus, Saint Paul, or the Book of Revelation talks about the afterlife. The most consistent metaphor of the Church – that is, all Christians everywhere – is as a bride getting ready for her wedding day.[192] The most consistent picture of what the fully realized Kingdom of God will look like is a huge banquet, often a wedding banquet. Jesus talks about this.[193] Saint Paul talks about this.[194] The Book of Revelation, in fact, paints the most vivid imagery of this:

> *"Hallelujah! For the Lord our God the Almighty reigns. Let us rejoice and exult and give him the glory, for the marriage of the Lamb has come, and his Bride has made herself ready; it was granted her to clothe herself with fine linen, bright and pure'— for*

---

[190] Mathew. 5:29-30, 7:13-14, 10:28, 13:42, 50, 18:9, 23:33, 25:46; Mark 9:43, 47-48; Luke 16:23

[191] Matthew 16:7; Romans 2:6-1; 1 Corinthians 3:14

[192] Revelation 21:2

[193] Matthew 22:1-14

[194] Ephesians 5:22-27

the fine linen is the righteous deeds of the saints. And the angel said to me, 'Write this: Blessed are those who are invited to the marriage supper of the Lamb.'[195] Come, I will show you the Bride, the wife of the Lamb.' And he carried me away in the Spirit to a great, high mountain, and showed me the holy city Jerusalem coming down out of heaven from God."[196]

Even the Book of Revelation, the same book of the Bible that mentions "lakes of fire," is more thematically focused on the "marriage supper" between "the Lamb" (that is, Jesus) and "the Bride" (that is, the Church). The consistency of this metaphor in the Bible should throw our popular conceptions of Heaven and hell into confusion. Why? A wedding ceremony, and a wedding party, is a wholly different dynamic than a system of reward for good people and punishment for bad people.

You see, if Heaven and hell is about reward or punishment, it doesn't make much sense that relatively immoral people would get rewarded with Heaven. It makes even less sense that relatively moral people would get punished with hell. If, however, the future inhabitants of Heaven are described as a bride getting ready for her wedding day, then this question of Heaven or hell isn't fundamentally about good people or bad people, and it isn't fundamentally about reward or punishment.

Heaven and hell are, most essentially, culminations of an ongoing relationship or the absence of it. Just as a wedding and marriage could be understood as "reward" for the courtship for two lovers, it is really the fitting culmination of the trajectory of their relationship. So too are Heaven and hell the fitting culmination of the trajectories you or I have desired.

---

[195] Revelation 19:6-9
[196] Revelation 21:9b-10

Have we desired relationship with God? Then we shall finally be united with God. Or have we desired anything less than God? Then we shall finally be apart from God. Heaven and hell are meant to honor those desires.

Hell may be an other-dimensional place, or it may be the absence of any place. Hell may be populated with souls of eternal regret, or it may mean the complete cessation of consciousness. Some progressive Christians even hope that hell would ultimately be emptied and every soul reconciled to God.[197] Christians throughout history have come to different conclusions based on the mixed metaphors of final judgment found in the Bible.

There also may be a punitive component to hell as well, as it is unavoidable to read Scripture and deny that God cares about justice.[198] Appropriate justice against the harm, evil, and idolatry committed by humanity will be fairly meted out by God in the end, but any justice administered by God before or during hell must be understood as a secondary effect rather than the primary goal of honoring the choice to be without God.

So if we are to be judged on anything by God, first and foremost it will be how we responded with faith to the offer of relationship from God. This also means that those who have never been explicitly exposed to Christianity are not inevitably without hope. Just as the ancient, Judaic forerunner Abraham responded to God with faith, Saint Paul says his response to God was sufficient for reconciliation, even though Abraham knew nothing of the Bible, the gospel, Jesus, or even a future messiah.[199]

---

[197] This belief about the salvation of all people is called "Christian universalism." It was held by some prominent early Christian leaders, but was eventually declared a heresy, or outside the spectrum of acceptable beliefs, by the Church at the Second Council of Constantinople in 553 CE.

[198] Isaiah 31:2; Romans 12:19; Revelation 21:8

[199] Galatians 3:6-9

This is not to say a person's moral performance or devoutness to their respective religion justifies them, for this would just be another variant of a good people versus bad people dichotomy. It is always Christ's atoning work on the cross that makes reconciliation possible across time and space. Only the atonement has the power to reach retroactively to a time without the gospel and proactively to those spaces without the gospel. If someone of another religion is reconciled to God through Christ, it will only be because they desired relationship with divine truth.[200]

Under these conditions, the majority of Christian traditions would agree that salvation is possible to those unreached by the Church, as a hidden extension of the Kingdom of God. To the extent people trust in those dimensions of their religion that reflect the truth that God pursues relationship out of sheer grace and mercy, we can have reasonable hope for their reconciliation to God.

Still, it is important not to confuse God's "Plan B" for God's "Plan A." This in no way negates the need for missionaries, since a well-contextualized gospel message is far more efficacious in helping people reconcile with God than being forced to rummage alone through one's non-Christian religion for piecemeal bits of saving truth. Likewise, few people in Western countries will fall under such an alternative metric, as if they did not have ample access to the gospel message or were presented with such a horrid distortion of Christianity that they were honestly unable to see its true nature. For the foreseeable future in the West, the eternal destiny of people will almost always be decided by a conscious acceptance or rejection of Christ's offer of relationship.

This, I believe, actually becomes a liberating truth upon deeper reflection. I should not – but more importantly cannot

---

[200] 2 Thessalonians 2:10b

– scare, manipulate, guilt, or bribe others into Heaven. The hope for the future that the Christian faith looks to is not a mercenary reward for the righteous and condemnation for those who couldn't make themselves sufficiently devout. We must never lose sight of the biblical imagery of romance that the Holy Spirit provided, otherwise our human propensity to make faith about checking religious boxes of proper belief and behavior will draw us away from the unexpected truth about Heaven and hell. Heaven will be the beginning of the great marriage between Christ and his lover and hell will be great estrangement between Christ and those who scorned his love.

This relational dynamic means hell – total separation from God – actually *must* exist for God to truly be a God of love. For this love to be genuine, God cannot force anyone into relationship with Godself, much less an eternal marriage. Love can never be forced. That is just as much an abuse as using the fear of hell to coerce belief or conformity. As much as we may like the idea of Heaven, we actually need to have hell so that a person's choice to not be in relationship with God can be respected.

This should not make us comfortable with hell, since even though it will not be a fiery torture pit, utter separation from the truth, beauty, joy, and love of God will be an unquestionable tragedy. Now, however, our discomfort should no longer exist out of fear or suspicion that God is unloving or lacking compassion. God loved the world unto death. God had such compassion for people that it took God to a cross. Any discomfort we feel about knowing people are on a trajectory to hell is the loving and compassionate Spirit of God convicting us to be equally loving and compassionate.

Motivated by what Christ has already done for us, we must live with the future in mind. We must live in such a way that when the day of the wedding finally arrives, we will be able to say that our conduct and our words gave our friends and loved ones every possible chance to say "yes" to Christ's marriage proposal.

So What? Trusting in the Hope for the Future

The closer the future is on our personal horizon, the better we are at responding to it. If I see a car barreling towards me as I cross the road, I very quickly realize I need to get out of its way. In contrast, the further the future is from us, the slower and less resolved our response. A whistle floating along on a railroad from an unseen train may not move us at all, even though we logically believe what the future will be like coming down the tracks.

The same challenge exists in trusting the future hope of the Christian faith. If we could know when the world was ending and that Christ was returning next week, most of us would quickly respond accordingly. However, since the future hope that awaits us at Christ's return, or at our own death, feels so far on our personal horizon, it is often very difficult to make today's and tomorrow's choices framed with such a seemingly distant hope.

Sometimes it may feel as if the return of Christ – the great marriage and the great estrangement, and the merging of Heaven and Earth – may never come.

Some Christians have tried to counteract this tendency by convincing themselves that the end is not distant, but actually very near. Growing up, most of my relatives and family believed that the world was coming to dramatic end within our lifetime. Some had specific dates, which seemed odd to me since Jesus told his followers that "no one knows the day or hour" of the end of the world.[201] Other relatives were looking for unusual geopolitical events to take place, or a charismatic but secretly sinister politician to be elected.

---

[201] Matthew 24:36

Unsurprisingly, I have yet to see an American president elected that wasn't accused by some group of being the harbinger of the biblical apocalypse.

While the intention to be more faithful is good, I have not seen this kind of approach play out well. Apart from simply being wrong – many apocalypse "dates" have come and gone quietly and all American presidents have disappointed critics when they failed to take over the world as the Anti-Christ – believing that the end of the world is right around the corner tends to create troublesome levels of worry. Perhaps worse, it distorts our view of culture and politics as utterly unredeemable, and so Christians cease to be viewed as a movement of hope and more as a movement of fear and condemnation.

Trusting in the hope for the future really asks us to be willing to live in the tension that the Second Coming of Christ may be tomorrow or that Christ may not return for another ten thousand years. Both may be true, and since we do not know which it is, we must be willing to ask ourselves if our lives can reflect a faithful response to either time of Christ's return.

If the world ended tomorrow – in Christ's return or in my untimely death – could I say that I faithfully used enough of this short time given to me? If you're wondering what "enough" looks like, there is perhaps an applicable story that Jesus tells where a poor man is invited to a lavish party, but is kicked out for not dressing appropriately.[202] We have all felt the flushed-cheek feeling of being woefully underdressed for the occasion. So if the thought of Christ returning tomorrow wouldn't make you feel embarrassed and panicked about what you have done and left undone, then perhaps we can say you are currently living with a healthy sense of urgency.

---

[202] Matthew 22:11-14

Of course, there is always more that could be done, but God is not asking us to be the *best*-dressed person at the party. God is simply asking us to respect the nature of the occasion. We have undeservedly been given a formal invitation to attend the party to top all parties. How could I not want to prepare for it properly? In proportion to my abilities and resources, I want to make the most of honoring this invitation as Christ's esteemed guest.

Still, if the world ended ten-thousand years from now, or if I lived far longer than I ever expected to, could I also say my life reflected an unusual level of emotional stability in an unstable world? Jesus told his disciples that many people after him will falsely declare the apocalypse is at hand. We might imagine this as a warning about religious people, which is applicable, but secular people have their own apocalypses that we must be careful to not get caught up with in the panic. That is, when those non-Christians around you are acting as if the world is coming to an end – because of an election loss, or stock market crash, or potential war – will people notice that strangely enough, you're *not* panicking?

It's not that we stand aloof or indifferent to personal or cultural calamity. Crises still require a response. Tragedy still warrants grieving. However, Saint Paul said that though we mourn, our mourning is different than those who do not have the same hope in Christ. [203] In every situation, I want to respond with a confidence that reflects faith in who is truly sovereign over the world. Afflictions cannot crush us or drive us to despair, for we believe that the unseen power of God is still relentlessly at work. [204]

Our hope for the future means trusting that God will make everything right at just the right time.

---

[203] 1 Thessalonians 4:13
[204] 2 Corinthians 4:8-9

A Beautiful Perseverance

Between Christ's first and second coming, we now live in two overlapping worlds of what the Christian faith calls the "now-and-not-yet," In one sense, because of the life, death, and resurrection of God, everything has changed for the better. This is the "now" part. In another sense, nothing has been perfected. This is the "not yet" part.

Jesus told his followers that the Kingdom of God was inaugurated with him, but that his kingdom is like an invasive garden weed. It will persevere and one day get into everything, but it is starting from very modest origins – a single seed.[205]

In the meantime, life is still hard for most of us. Loved ones still get sick. Debt still piles up. People still die. My sins still tempt me. Where can we find the strength to press on?

Harriet Tubman escaped from slavery in 1849 from her Maryland plantation into the free state of Pennsylvania. Even though this new freedom put "glory in everything" and felt "like Heaven," there was still a major problem. Almost all of Tubman's family were still enslaved. In perhaps the most enrapturing but also painful of ways, she was living in a now-and-not-yet reality. It is both Tubman's decisiveness and perseverance that stands out. Tubman, whose faith had been rooted in her since she was a little girl, was comfortable talking with God.

She later recounted, "I said to the Lord, I'm going to hold steady on to you, and I know you will see me through... and I prayed to God to make me strong and able to fight, and that's what I've always prayed for ever since." [206] Despite being plagued by frequent bouts of illness, Harriet Tubman made thirteen trips back to Maryland to free seventy other people from slavery, including her family. During the American Civil

---

[205] Matthew 13:31-32
[206] Harriet Tubman to Ednah Dow Cheney, 1865

War, she assisted the Union Army in freeing at least seven hundred more.

Even after the Civil War, Tubman continued to work towards women's suffrage. Still, the world never became perfect. In spite of her being often plagued by debilitating bad health, Tubman joyously lived in the tension of the now-and-not-yet kingdom. Her sense of this, without fancy theological language, is still clear.

She reflected, "God's time is always near. He set the North Star in the heavens; He gave me the strength in my limbs; He meant I should be free."[207] Her understanding of God's time – God's way and will for our lives – being always near, shows us that even when we feel like we are experiencing "not yet," God's "now" is still near.

This is true as well for our struggles to overcome sin. John Newton was a sailor in the eighteenth century, when his ship almost sank. Despite his previous dislike of Christianity and an indulgent lifestyle that had spiraled out of control, he prayed aloud to God for rescue. The ship somehow drifted safely ashore, and Newton soon became a Christian.

However, Newton was also involved in the slave trade, eventually captaining multiple slave ships. His Christian conversion, while it reformed his personal moral behavior in many ways, did not open his eyes to the evils of slavery, much less cause him to jettison all his sins. His internal spiritual life was both "now" and "not yet," reflecting a sanctification process that was immediate in its start but woefully shallow in its depth. Newton persevered though in letting God change more and more of his life.

Eventually, Newton was convicted to give up his business with the slave trade and became a minister, despite much opposition from the Church of England. Years later he

---

[207] Harriet Tubman to Ednah Dow Cheney, New York City, circa 1859.

would write to British parliament about his past sin with "a confession, which ... comes too late ... It will always be a subject of humiliating reflection to me, that I was once an active instrument in a business at which my heart now shudders."[208] Newton went on to become the leading abolitionist in England and witnessed the end of the slave trade in the British Empire.

Given the depths of depravity John Newton came from, his sense of personal now-and-not-yet shows a level of self-awareness that goes beyond typical spiritual piety. Writing later in his life, Newton would proclaim, "I am not what I ought to be – ah, how imperfect and deficient! I am not what I wish to be – I abhor what is evil, and I would cleave to what is good! I am not what I hope to be – soon, soon shall I put off mortality, and with mortality all sin and imperfection. Yet, though I am not what I ought to be, nor what I wish to be, nor what I hope to be, I can truly say, I am not what I once was; a slave to sin and Satan; and I can heartily join with the apostle, and acknowledge, 'By the grace of God I am what I am."[209] No wonder he could also write the hymn, *Amazing Grace*.

Both Harriet Tubman and John Newton, the escaped slave and the slave trader, vividly experienced the now-and-not-yet kingdom in their lives. While one needed courage to defeat injustice and the other needed conviction to repent of his perpetuation of injustice, both experienced the persevering power that comes from having a hope for the future. The Christian faith believes that God's presence did not just exist in the past, but is near today and will come in fullness at Christ's return. That assurance of God's ultimate sovereignty in the present and the future gives us hope that we can

---

[208] John Newton, *Thoughts upon the African Slave Trade* (London: Printed for J. Buckland, and J. Johnson, 1788, p. 2)

[209] John Newton and Josiah Bull, *Letters by the Rev. John Newton of Olney and St. Mary Woolnoth* (London: Religious Tract Society, 1869, p. 400).

accomplish what we otherwise could not if our fate was purely random or a matter of insurmountable odds.

Tubman persevered, with God helping her to destroy chattel slavery in her land and save her family. Newton persevered, with God helping him to destroy the slave trade in his land and save what was once a deadened conscience. Whether it be external challenges or internal struggles, God has not given up on you. God's time is near, and God desires to do equally beautiful things in you.

FAITH HOPE LOVE

CHAPTER SEVEN
Love For The World

The incarnation, death, and resurrection of God was the fulcrum of the human story. A high-water mark of drama where God turned back relational brokenness, injustice, corruption, and death once and for all. Estrangement has been overcome by the reconciling love of God. Still, the skeptic might object with the obvious and undeniable observation, "Then why is there so much of all that terrible stuff still around?" It's a good question.

This isn't so much of a theodicy problem about the benevolent nature of God, that is, a question of God's love or goodness. We already know that while terrible and seemingly inexplicable suffering does exist in the world, God willingly entered into that suffering alongside us. The cross of Christ proved the love of the Triune God. The stubbornness of sin in the world though raises doubts about the *omnipotence* of the

Triune God. If the resurrection was the battle that turned the metaphysical tide of a cosmic war, why hasn't the world gotten better yet? There are two responses to this confusion.

First, it would be incorrect to say that the world hasn't gotten better. Many religions and even more news outlets like to push a narrative that society is spiraling out of control, or that we'll be living in some post-apocalyptic wasteland one generation from now. This narrative, however, relies on cherry-picking data and fearmongering. By nearly every conceivable marker, the world is better now than it was two-thousand years ago and better than it was even a hundred years ago. There is less war, disease, and starvation than ever before in human history. Even terrorism and genocide, as terrible as that has been in the twentieth and twenty-first centuries, pales in comparison to the slaughters of centuries and millennia past.[210]

If it seems that the world is not getting any better (and perhaps worse), it's only because our globalized media make us more *aware* of suffering on a global scale more than any time in human history. Admittedly, while our runaway carbon emissions and degradation of the environment threaten to undermine our progress, according to objective data, human suffering and evil is gradually on the global retreat.[211]

The Kingdom of God and Christ's Church

It can be debated, however, how much this progress has anything to do with Christ's victory in his resurrection. Maybe all this human progress is instead simply the result of market

---

[210] For example, the Mongol invasions in the 13th and 14th centuries killed up to 11% of the world's entire population.

[211] Max Roser, "The short history of global living conditions and why it matters that we know it" Our World in Data, https://ourworldindata.org/a-history-of-global-living-conditions-in-5-charts.

forces, reason, and science? This, of course, naively assumes such things are not gifts of God that are meant to be used by God's people for good, but this first answer is not meant to be our primary answer, anyway. The second and more important response for why the world has indeed gotten better since Christ's resurrection is that the Kingdom of God has spread to every nation on earth and to more unique people groups than any other religion, ideology, or social movement in history.[212] Wherever the Kingdom of God has advanced, so has the reconciling love of God.

Countless lives have not only been saved from the hell of spiritual death, but have received radical restoration in this life. Entire cultures were moved to value the sanctity of human life more, like ending infanticide and developing public health care. They have also seen their systems that exploited human life overthrown, like abolishing slavery and caste systems and advancing women's equality.[213] Where the Kingdom of God has gone, the gates of hell have not only failed to prevail against the Kingdom, but the Kingdom has tunneled underneath the gates themselves and wreaked glorious havoc with the power of Christ's love. In this way, the world has gotten immeasurably better since the incarnation, death, and resurrection of God. Saint Paul says that this is central to our life's mission as followers of Jesus. He says we are meant to be "ambassadors of reconciliation."[214]

You might think I've been describing the last two-thousand years of Christian history with naïve rose-colored lenses and choosing to ignore all the darker periods of crusades and inquisitions. However, there is an important distinction that must be drawn here. We should be careful not to conflate

---

[212] The Joshua Project (joshuaproject.net) estimates that Christianity has developed a sustainable presence in approximately 10,000 of the world's 17,000 unique people groups.
[213] Some elements of Christianity in the West have indeed internalized sexism and patriarchy, but this is a historical aberration compared to historic and global Christianity.
[214] 2 Corinthians 5:20

the *Kingdom* with the *Church*. The Kingdom is invisible, with boundaries that cannot easily be defined by human judgments. The Church is visible, with boundaries defined by human institutions.

Without this distinction, we might become disillusioned. Wherever the Church has been, it has brought with it great good and reconciling power, but sometimes also great evil and corruption. Why? Imperfect people always create imperfect institutions. In fact, there has never been a time in human history where the institutions of God's people, be they in the Old Testament or the New Testament, haven't been in need of serious reform.

There have also always been, either out of malice or ignorance, frauds and fakes in those institutions. People who wore the uniform, but had no real affection for the team or coach. Jesus, knowing how hard it is for these kind of people to be identified by their contemporaries, called this spiritual phenomenon "the tares among the wheat."[215] As it turns out, the tares in first-century Palestine were almost indistinguishable from the wheat they grew among. You were just as likely to weed out the wheat by accident.

The Kingdom, on the other hand, not only exists within the institutional Church in those faithfully following the way of Jesus, but also those outside of it. The Kingdom happens when the will of God breaks into the world, and this can be experienced by both Christians and non-Christians. The Bible has many stories of the Holy Spirit at work outside of institutional frameworks, and always much to the surprise of the people within the religious institution![216] These extra-institutional manifestations of God's presence do not happen in opposition to the institutional Church, as if no Church is ever needed. Rather, they function both to draw new people

---

[215] Matthew 13:24-30
[216] For example, Numbers 11:26-30, Numbers 22, and Acts 10:28-35.

into Christian community and to provide ever-necessary reform to those Christian communities.

The Mission of the Church

If your identity is now with Christ as an adopted child of God, your mission is now Christ's mission. What is this mission? Jesus described his mission in two complementary ways. First, in Luke's gospel, Jesus declares to a crowd after reading from an ancient prophet, "The Spirit of the Lord is upon me, because he has anointed me to proclaim good news to the poor. He has sent me to proclaim liberty to the captives and recovery of sight to the blind, to set at liberty those who are oppressed."[217] This is a radical mission!

It is important we not misunderstand Jesus' description of this mission too literally, as if Jesus is advocating a political uprising and regular miraculous healings of blind people. Later on in Luke's same story, Jesus also says of his mission, "For the Son of Man came to seek and to save the lost."[218] Jesus is not searching for people who have lost their map. Jesus is pursuing all who have been estranged from God in order to bring us back into relationship with God. Jesus's mission then, contextually understood, is both social and spiritual.

Christians, historically, have struggled with this tension. Those from more progressive traditions have tended to focus on the social implications of Jesus' message to the exclusion of an individual's need to be reconciled from their estrangement to God. These churches preach political revolution without addressing the dire spiritual needs of the world. Conversely, those from more conservative traditions have tended to focus on the spiritual implication of Jesus'

---

[217] Luke 4:18
[218] Luke 19:10

message to the exclusion of working towards justice for the marginalized and oppressed. These churches preach spiritual salvation without addressing the dire social inequalities of the world.

Jesus, on the other hand, says his mission and our mission is to serve as ambassadors of reconciliation that will bring people from spiritual death to life and from oppression to liberty. What's more, both are mutually supportive of one another. The Christian who socially embodies "good news" for those in need will make the "good news" of spiritual reconciliation with God coherent and consistent. Likewise, the story of spiritual reconciliation achieved by Christ and the commands of the Bible on behalf of the marginalized and oppressed gives profound moral grounding to a political system awash with identity politics and power plays.

Is this truly *our* mission though? Perhaps it was Christ's mission, but how do we know it has been passed down to us? We know because after his resurrection, Jesus appeared to his disciples and commissioned them, saying, "All authority in heaven and on earth has been given to me. Go therefore and make disciples of all nations, baptizing them in the name of the Father and of the Son and of the Holy Spirit, teaching them to observe all that I have commanded you. And behold, I am with you always, to the end of the age."[219]

In what is popularly known as the *Great Commission*, the risen Jesus tells his disciples to go and make more disciples, who will make more disciples, and so on, all the way down to us. The mission Jesus gave to the first disciples had been carried faithfully forward by the Church for two millennia to you and me. The Great Commission has at times been conflated with European colonialism or American "Manifest Destiny," but this was a theological hijacking permitted by the

---

[219] Matt. 18:6-20

imperial kind of Christianity that prevailed at the time. Christianity was founded not as a faith of the colonizer (Rome), but of the colonized (occupied Judea).

In fact, the Great Commission is really a continuation of the covenant and commission of Abraham by God to make him a "blessing to all families on the earth" back in the Hebrew Book of Genesis. God charges this nomadic herder, "I will make you into a great people, and I will bless you. I will make your name great, *so* that you will be a blessing."[220] It moves from the bottom-up and from the margins-in. Our mission is that ancient and magnificent, but it is also humbled by the awareness that its future is utterly dependent on God and not on human institutions. Christ has given the mission, but he will also see to its success.

The Uniqueness of Christian Community

Still, if churches have their obvious blemishes, not to mention those churches which fail entirely to either share the gospel of spiritual salvation or fail to carry out into culture the gospel's obvious social implications, do we really need then to be part of a church? Can't we participate in Christ's mission outside of the organized Church?

Throughout history, there have been points where Christians have opted out of traditional participation in churches. However, this was not to avoid spiritual and moral commitments, but to add more. In times of malaise in the Church, men and women joined Christian communes with the goal of devoting one's entire life to God through rhythmic prayer, fasting, and work. Spiritual ascetics living in caves notwithstanding, there are no examples of notable, isolated Christians in history or in the Bible.

---

[220] Gen. 12:2-2

Perhaps to the chagrin of modern Western people, the idea that one can be a Christian without community is something of an oxymoron. For better or for worse, we are stuck with our churches. Or, more colorfully put by the social activist and Christian convert Dorothy Day, "The church may be a harlot at times, but she is my mother."[221]

So what can we do? Join one. Not passively, or as a consumer of religious goods and services, but as someone who desires to change the world with Christ and through Christ. This doesn't mean we should compromise our integrity for the sake of supposedly "fitting in" with a given church. The local church and the wider Church needs faithful reformers that aren't going anywhere. You are able to help make the Church more faithful to Christ's mission.

Besides, no charity, political party, or social movement is perfect, and yet many of us gladly participate in them because we know great good can be achieved when we work together. Even with all the problems we might be able to point out in churches, the Church has been formed by Christ to be the embassy from where we serve as ambassadors of reconciliation. No ambassador can work effectively, perhaps even legitimately, without an embassy. Why should I think that I am somehow the exception?

The Church also serves as the locus for something truly unique that cannot be accomplished outside of Church – facilitating communal worship of the Triune God. It is, at least by now, a cliché when someone explains why they don't attend church by objecting, "I can worship God outside in nature." Of course God can be worshiped anywhere. The entirety of creation speaks to God's glory.[222] Nature would cry out if we

---

[221] Dorothy Day, "In Peace Is My Bitterness Most Bitter," *The Catholic Worker*, January 1967, 1-2.
[222] Psalms 19:1-4; Romans 1:20

were silent,[223] and yet, our souls need a kind of worship that is more specific than looking at a sunset.

Worshiping with other Christians is crucial for spiritual flourishing because is an act meant to shape the curvature of the soul. My soul's default tendency is to bend inward on myself and focus on my own concerns, plans, and wants. Even an otherwise religious person will drift towards spiritual navel-gazing with too much solitary devotion. Worship, like a morning stretch upon waking from bed, is meant to draw our posture out and our gaze up.

During worship the hymns and songs bring our minds to reflect on God's love through creation, but also God's love from Heaven and God's love for the world. Sermons teach us what God did in the past and rekindle the hope of what God will do in the future. Receiving communion unites us with all Christians symbolically and mystically with the presence of Christ. Baptism seals us as part of the covenant family of God and requires all who participate to promise one another fidelity and love. Worship, as practiced by a church, is designed to curve my soul outward toward God and my neighbor like nothing else can.

This isn't to say worship can't feel unexciting, boring, or serious at times. In fact, the seriousness of encountering the Source-of-All-Existence should possess at least some weight that differentiates worship from feeling like a motivational seminar. Glory, however one measures it, is a heavy thing. Worship that constantly seeks to entertain quickly loses a sense of sacredness.

This also isn't to say worship can't feel weird sometimes. In some ways worship *should* feel weird since we do it so little. While I am often guilty of implicitly worshiping what is less than God, even the most wayward version of myself

---

[223] Isaiah 55:12; Luke 19:37-40

knows better than to explicitly worship people or things in my day-to-day life. Irreligious people sense this as well, seeming to intuitively know the psychological power and meaning of worship and taking care not to do it. Worshiping the Triune God – Father, Son, and Holy Spirit – Creator, Redeemer, Sustainer – should feel like nothing else we do, because nothing else but the Triune God is worthy of something as strange as worship.

Though the Kingdom of God exists as a phenomenon larger than the Church, the Church has been elected by God to reveal a glimpse of the fully-realized will of God on earth. This mission is accomplished by a rhythm of gathering and scattering. Gathered, church communities come together to be equipped by worship. Once equipped, they are scattered back out into the world, only to return once more. When we join this rhythm, we are no longer just moving to the beat of our own spiritual drum, but playing a faithful part in God's symphony.

Loving the World as God Does

The mission of God is big, so big that when you start to take in all that God wants to do, and how God is asking you to play a part in it all, it can quickly feel overwhelming. This feeling points to another blessing that comes from life in a church community. Surrounded by an adoptive spiritual family, it is not up to you alone to attempt to love the world as God does.

Christ has called us into a community of people with individual abilities and resources pooled together. Saint Paul uses the analogy of individual body parts working together for the functioning of the whole body. [224] Together, a church celebrates communion and baptism as a way to unify the body

---

[224] 1 Corinthians 12:27

and receive outpourings of grace. A church, even an very flawed one, is where we learn how to pray to God and how to listen for the will of God. It is where we go to be encouraged as well as challenged to repent of those sins we have rationalized away. Like the Trinity, Christian community, at its best, is marked by the giving and receiving of love that overflows into the world.

Christians have a common phrase you may have heard before, "Be in the world, but not of the world." This comes from a prayer that Jesus prayed over his disciples shortly before his arrest and execution,[225] because he wanted his disciples to strike a difficult balance. On one hand, he did not want us becoming self-righteous ascetics living supposedly pure and holy lives apart from the dirty and corrupt culture. Religious people do that kind of thing all the time, and while they might feel good about this separation, this behavior does little to change the world. On the other hand, he did not want us becoming complicit contributors to a culture that did not love God or love their neighbor. Religious people do this as well, pretending to be spiritual, but really adopting all the same unhealthy behaviors as anyone else in their culture.

When John's gospel account references God's love for the world, it is important to realize that this is a love which neither approves of the culture nor washes its hands of it. Perhaps the most famous verse in the Bible is found where John quotes Jesus as saying, "For God so loved the world that he gave his only Son, that whoever believes in him should not perish but have eternal life."[226] This love does not condemn the world, but graciously subverts it that others might see a better way – God's way of following Jesus and experiencing the fullness of life offered by him. We are meant to display love for the world in the same way God already does.

---

[225] John 17:15
[226] John 3:16

Still, because the Kingdom of God is difficult to definitively define and God's plan for the world's redemption is so grand in scope, it is understandable to be confused about what it could look like to partner with what God is already doing. Is this something I can be doing, practically speaking, in my daily life? A helpful starting point is to recall the four categories of existence ruined by sin, and then begin to imagine what life would look like if they began to slowly reverse. This is the eternal life Jesus refers to.

So, for those in Christian community, we should be working towards restoring broken relationships. This begins with constantly renewing our relationship with the Triune God, since God is the only true source of healing. Flowing out of that restoration, we are empowered to relate to sin in a different way. Rather than hating sinners and loving my own sin, as I am naturally prone to do, I can now love sinners and hate my own sin.[227] With my heart enlarged and my pride diminished by the work of God's Spirit, I can then assist in healing others even as I find healing within my own psyche. On a larger-scale, this can mean participating in mission work at home and abroad, as well as being peacemakers in our families and communities. On a smaller-scale, this means inviting friends and loved ones to experience reconciliation with God, and helping others to conquer their shame with grace.

Of course, not every relationship will be mended and we will likely never heal all our personal neuroses, but since we believe that God loves the world, God will restore relationally all that can possibly be restored.

Of perhaps a second order, but no less important, the Christian community is meant to be an agent of justice and mercy for our neighbors. This may mean using existing power

---

[227] Let us also avoid the phrase, "Hate the sin, love the sinner." It's cliché and typically demeaning.

structures to humbly create new laws that give equality to the oppressed and give full dignity to the marginalized, or it may be speaking truth to power outside of traditional politics. On a smaller-scale, it may be contributing and shaping a local economy that does not privilege one ethnic group or socio-economic class over another. Even how and who we vote for can reflect this calling to extend justice and mercy.

We should not delude ourselves by thinking that we can bring Heaven to earth by way of politics or that our laws can be used to force citizens to act as pseudo-Christians. Many Christians have made this mistake in the past, and still do today. Instead, since we believe that God loves the world, the goal should be to create a foretaste of what God will do. We anticipate that one day the full justice of God will see every oppressor repent or be toppled, every ethnicity celebrated, and every person will be fully respected as wonderfully made in the image of God.

Where we have corrupted our environment, the Christian community can be an active participant in helping renew our ecosystems by supporting policies that protect our water and air and invests in renewable sources of energy. On a smaller-scale, we can contribute as we feel convicted to be faithful stewards of the earth by choosing sustainable farming, more humane raising of livestock, or plant-based diets. Recycling and decreasing our consumption, when done mindfully as a practice of loving the world as God does, may be no less part of your ongoing discipleship than reading Scripture. Even treating our bodies as wonderfully-made vessels bestowed with the *imago Dei* can direct us away from the socially-induced excesses of both vanity and gluttony, and instead set us on the path of holistic health.

We know that we alone cannot save the planet, nor can we stave off every disease by good exercise, but since we believe that God loves the world, one day God will create harmony between all of creation and the diseases that have ravaged us will be no more.

Now all that being said, there's not much we can do about death. Currently, the human mortality rate stands at 100%. We might say that we can honor God's plan to undo death by minimizing killing in the world. However, if we are already participating in the restoration of broken relationships by peacemaking and working toward justice and mercy, we should already be working to reduce both individual and state-sanctioned killing in the world.

Essentially, it is a question we need to constantly ask ourselves to help reframe our perspective in a culture that excuses the killing of people when it is profitable or convenient. On any given issue, I should ask, "How does what I say or do contribute to a culture that honors the sacredness of life?" Asking this question of ourselves, it will inevitably put us at odds with different elements of our culture, both political conservatives and political liberals. Despite this inevitable tension, it will always be worth asking, for it challenges us to be Kingdom-backed agents of a holy subversion against the political, social, and economic systems that have little interest in protecting the most vulnerable.

Let's not kid ourselves, either. We never really save lives. We only postpone deaths. While we may create precious delays, there is nothing we can do to halt the inevitable march of death. So in a way, that commonplace wish so many people have for life after death is not misplaced. Since God loves the world, one day the Author of life will reverse death itself. Not just for our bodies, nor even those loved ones we wish to see again, but for the entire cosmos.

This alludes to the fundamental difference between how a secular person and a Christian understand the nature of doing good. Secular people often wonder if their acts of charity and justice are viewed by Christians as less valid. They should not be. Doing good is always good, regardless of who is doing it. However, secular people do deny themselves the immense benefit of knowing what their positive contributions will lead to.

Imagine two people planting a handful of garden seeds. The first person plants seeds because they enjoy doing it. They may even look forward to what it grows into and feeding people with the produce. This person also realizes, in their more honest moments though, that one day weeds will overtake their tiny garden. The second person plants seeds not only out of enjoyment, but because they believe they are part of cultivating the beginning of what will one day be a thriving farm. Both plant seeds and their planting is equally valid. Both will hope for growth and to feed others and their desires are equally noble. The Christian, however, plants seeds with a vision that God will take every seed and use them for something far grander than what could ever be grown on a tiny patch of dirt and in a finite amount of time. Those few seeds, faithfully sown, will become part of an unending harvest that will feed more people than the farmer will ever know.

Understanding the good we contribute to the world as being woven into a redemptive tapestry that will last forever is deeply satisfying. It can certainly prompt people to work for positive change, both large and small, who might have otherwise grown cynical by the logical implications of believing nothing will truly last. Perhaps more practically, it can also provide a sense of patience and serenity in the good we are attempting to do, trusting that it is not up to *me* to solve every problem *now*. I can have confidence that my contribution will make a difference, even if I cannot live to see it come to fruition.

In the end, God's love wins in every way, whether we are aware of it or whether we believe it. Moreover, we have been given the special invitation to become one of the many extensions of that love which will carry on – not just for years, generations, or millennia – but over and through eternity.

So What? Trusting in God's Love for the World

God's love may win in the end, but as we discussed earlier with the Christian hope for the future, the end may be – or feel – a long way off. Partnering with God to reverse the effects of sin and estrangement may sometimes feel costly, perhaps too costly. The right choice is often the hard choice, and it is difficult for a reason. How I can trust God when Jesus says this is the best way to live? It often doesn't seem that way.

People can be undeserving of your love. People can resist your love. People can hate your love. If all these things happened to Jesus, then you can expect that these things will happen to you, too.

Often, when we choose as Jesus did to restore relationships, resist injustice, honor God's creation, or combat a culture of death, we will be opposed.[228] When we suffer from this opposition, we are vicariously volunteering to absorb part of the effects of sin and estrangement. Without the work of Christ, we might be tempted to imagine ourselves atoning for the sins of the world, that our suffering from opposition to doing good justifies us as morally and ethically upright people. However, because Christ has already atoned for every sin of the past, present, and future, the cost we bear from loving the world as God does is not meant to prove ourselves to anyone. Loving the world as God does is our opportunity to share in the suffering of Christ.

Why would I want to share in Christ's suffering? Pragmatically speaking, it allows me to know what I truly believe. You believe nothing until you suffer for it. Suffering

---

[228] John 15:18

burns away my externalized and public beliefs and leaves my deepest internalized convictions. This process, as painful as it might be, makes us authentic people.

Still, the greatest reasoning for sharing in Christ's suffering is more direct. The first letter from Saint John to a Christian community said it so succinctly, that "We love because God first loved us."[229] When I was undeserving of God's love, Christ reached out to me. When I resisted God's love extended to me, Christ pursued me. When my broken moral compass of right and wrong led to the murder of the only perfect person on a cross, Christ forgave me. I trust that loving the world as God does is worthwhile despite the costs, because Christ considered loving me worthwhile despite the infinitely greater costs.

Yet we are not meant to suffer just for the sake of suffering. Saint Peter says our baptism in Christ is a sign of our solidarity with Christ, so to share in Christ's suffering is to share in his victory.[230] When I love the world as God does, even if it is personally or socially costly, this is an investment in the economy of God. It will be returned to me in full and with better interest than any stock exchange could offer me. When I love the world as God does, even when I seem to lose against more powerful forces at work, this for the Lord of Heaven's armies is a badge of courage. It will be a medal of honor bestowed on me better than any earthly distinction.

I can trust that loving the world the way God does will not be simplistic or easy, but that it will be proven worthwhile even when our most faithful attempts seem worthless. Successfully changing the world is ultimately God's responsibility and not our own, and so I can rest in the assurance that God is capable of using every offering of love for God's glory and my neighbors' good.

---

[229] 1 John 4:19
[230] 1 Peter 4:13

A Beautiful Ethic

Can people be good without God? Absolutely.

History is full of stories of heroic and noble acts by people who did not derive their ethical code from their belief in God, much less an understanding about the character of the Triune God. Yet, there is a myth perpetuated by some prideful religious people, but also some defensive irreligious people, that those who believe in God claim that a belief in God is necessary to be morally upstanding.

To be historically accurate, most of what we consider today in the West as attributes of a "good person" are derivatives of a Christian morality that have been sanitized with the Enlightenment. Philosophers of the Enlightenment retained most of the Christian ethics passed down by the Church, but attempted to detach them from their connection to the Triune God and replace them with a justification based on humanism or reason. Though the definition of a good person has always been something of a moving target based on culture and era, we can say that even the most ardent atheist who is considered a good person by modern Western society's standards owes their ethical code to a philosophical inheritance from the Christian faith.

Still, a cursory look at just about any character in the Bible should dispel this myth that a belief in God makes people good and a disbelief in God makes people bad. The Bible is full of terribly behaved believers while showcasing a handful of upstanding pagans. [231] Belief in God does not enable good behavior any more than disbelief in God inevitably creates bad behavior

Yet an ethical code that comes from a belief in God, and especially Christ, is fundamentally different in this respect; it believes its ethics are ultimately real, ultimately meaningful,

---

[231] Joshua 2:1-24; 2 Samuel 11:1-27

and ultimately inclusive. At the risk of being too simplistic, Enlightenment philosophers reduced what were previously Christian ethics to a Kantian inspired, but Hobbesian grounded "social contract."[232] For example, I do not steal from you because I do not want you to steal from me. We act ethically because it is in society's – really our own – best self-interest to do so. However, watch any dystopian or post-apocalyptic movie and you see how easily this contract can break down. Why? It's because while the social contract is real, the ethics themselves are not. If I can steal from you because I have a gun and I know I will not be held accountable, history shows us that all bets are off.

As the Nazis came to power in Germany, one of their early decrees was to require all churches to swear loyalty to Adolf Hitler and the Nationalist Socialist Party. Most religious people, wanting to be good German citizens, complied. A minority did not, even though it was in their every interest to do so. They were called "Confessing Churches," echoing the name given to those Christians – the "Confessors" – who were imprisoned and tortured by Roman authorities during the centuries when Christianity was illegal, yet did not recant their faith.

One such leader of this spiritual resistance was pastor and theologian, Dietrich Bonhoeffer. He used his eloquence through his writing and the radio to speak out against the Nazis. He was offered safe passage to the United States, but refused. Eventually, the Nazis captured Bonhoeffer and sent him to a concentration camp. Some sympathetic guards later offered him a chance to escape, but he also refused in order to protect his relatives from Nazi reprisals. He was executed two weeks before Allied troops liberated the camp.

---

[232] Immanuel Kant of the eighteenth century and Thomas Hobbes of the seventeenth century were both philosophers, with Kant representing to many human idealism and optimism and Hobbes symbolizing human pragmatism and pessimistic realism.

His last recorded words were to an English prisoner, "This is the end — for me the beginning of life."[233]

Even a Nazi doctor, who likely embellished much of his account of Bonhoeffer's death to appear more humane, could not help but admit, "In the almost fifty years that I worked as a doctor, I have hardly ever seen a man die so entirely submissive to the will of God."[234]

Living under the barbaric Nazi regime in Germany – though it was one of the most scientifically and intellectually advanced nations in the world – tore up much of the traditional social contract of the Enlightenment. As the German-American political philosopher Hannah Arendt documented in her book on rank-and-file Nazis, *Eichman in Jerusalem: A Report on the Banality of Evil,* otherwise morally upstanding people gradually found themselves participating in atrocities. What happened to most German churches and most German citizens should not surprise us. It is well-documented human behavior that beneath our veneer of respectability lurks the capacity for total depravity. Instead, what we should pay close attention to are those rare people in history who are able to maintain moral sight even after everyone else has gone blind.

How could someone like Bonhoeffer see through the corrupted ethics of German nationalism and anti-Semitism? Key to Bonhoeffer's moral clarity was that his ethics were not contingent upon a shifting cultural standard or social contract. He believed in a universal, transcendental good derived from God, and specifically Christ. This meant that, to him, his ethics were ultimately real. Even atheist philosophers acknowledge, sometimes triumphantly and other times reluctantly, that true

---

[233] Bethge, Eberhard. *Dietrich Bonhoeffer.* (München: Kaiser, 1981), 830

[234] Vincent Langlet and Victoria J. Barnett. *Dietrich Bonhoeffer: A Biography* (Minneapolis, MN: Fortress Press, 2000), 928.

good can only exist if God exists. If God does not exist, we become our own gods with our own culturally negotiated ethical codes.

I can certainly desire to be what I think is a "good person" without reference to God because it makes me feel good about myself, but I will be unable to know if my concept of good is nothing more than a socially conditioned construct. My ethical values will have no moral power beyond myself, and they will be so subjectively wrapped up with my own ego that it will be incredibly difficult to critique my own behavior beyond a vague personal sense of utilitarianism. To the extent that I choose this path, I am merely playing a great game of make-believe.

The Christian faith, however, offers a beautiful ethic based on Christ that is capable of critiquing all cultures and systems, even those associated with the Church and Christianity itself. In his essay *Ethics*, Bonhoeffer writes, "The subject matter of a Christian ethic is God's reality revealed in Christ becoming real among God's creatures."[235] It is an ethical system not subjectively dependent on itself, but rather on the revealed character of the Triune God demonstrated by Christ. This means I can logically critique not only problematic systems and behavior, but also my own life so that I might better myself.

Still, how could someone like Bonhoeffer uphold those universal convictions about right and wrong under the cost of torture and death? It is one thing to believe your ethics are true in all times and in all places, but it's another to be willing to die by them against an evil power that would wipe out even the very memory of your noble sacrifice. Bonhoeffer not only believed that the end of this life was not the end, but that his ethical choices were ultimately meaningful.

---

[235] Bonhoeffer, Dietrich, Clifford J. Green ,and Michael DeJonge, eds., *The Bonhoeffer Reader*. (Minneapolis: Fortress Press, 2014) 596.

Even if we believe our ethics are real, without God's plan to preserve and restore the world, our ethics are still meaningless. Every heroic and cowardly act, every deed of kindness and cruelty, will eventually be erased by the sands of time and the heat death of the universe. The greatest peacemakers and the most bloodthirsty dictators will all be slowly forgotten until there is no sentient being around to forget. Despite being well-versed in this atheistic possibility, Bonhoeffer chose to believe that Christ was the "crucified reconciler," initiating a reconciliation of all things. If it is true that our actions are part of the eternal drama of God, then every action and choice is bursting with ultimate meaning.

The Christian faith offers a beautiful ethic that can make meaning in the face of seeming meaninglessness. Instead of everything being forgotten, nothing will. The good we do in this life, even the good that is never written down, noticed, or remembered, will become part of God's cosmic redemption.[236]

When you have rock solid ethical convictions that you are willing to die by, it would be easy to condemn those who fail to share them, especially those who actively oppose them. After all, isn't that the same kind of radicalization that creates suicide bombers? In fact, this problem is not limited to religious radicals, but even people who would consider themselves entirely irreligious.

Ethical beliefs, whether they come from religion, philosophy, or political ideology, almost always possess a tendency to identify someone else as the "other" who is inferior to "you." This process of "othering" is based on where other people fail to meet your criteria of moral worth. It's not just wrong religious views that disqualify them. In our increasingly secular culture, it is someone's wrong political views that make them the "other."

---

[236] Psalm 139:1-6

Additionally, our own strong ethical codes contrasted with those who we think fall short provides a particularly satisfying psychological assurance that all people need. It is our need to justify our own value and worthiness before others. Religions, philosophies, and political ideologies assure me that I am a good person who can stand justified before the world, and that there are other people who are not good and cannot justify themselves like *I* can. In short, apart from making you arrogant and condescending, it also becomes exclusionary and condemning of anyone who does not fall into your "good" category.

And yet, Bonhoeffer did not develop this attitude towards his Nazi tormentors, believing that Christ died to save his enemies, and called his followers to do the same. Christianity has long held that there are no "good" people to begin with. We all fall short of the ethical standard that we could possibly hope to justify ourselves with.[237] Therefore, to exclude any person as unworthy of love – even our enemies – is to exclude ourselves too. To condemn anyone as irredeemable – even those we believe are making the world worse – is to condemn ourselves.

The Christian faith offers a beautiful ethic based on Christ that is inclusive of offering grace to all people, and seeing even enemies as potential friends, but without losing its commitment to the good.[238] When practiced faithfully and thoughtfully, it is a way of life that can reverberate in subtle revolutions, both across the dinner table and around the world.

---

[237] Psalm 53:3; Romans 3:23
[238] Matthew 5:43-48; Titus 3:3-8; 1 John 2:2

FAITH HOPE LOVE

CHAPTER EIGHT
The Response

A young boy lay dying of cancer in an East Tennessee hospital a few weeks before Christmas. He wanted to see Santa Claus, so a local Santa actor suited up. A war veteran with a long white beard, he was unprepared for what was about to happen.

When he walked in, the boy was lying there. He was so weak it looked as if he was about to fall asleep. Santa sat down on the bed and asked, "Say, what's this I hear about you're gonna miss Christmas? There's no way you can miss Christmas! Why, you're my Number One elf!"

The gaunt boy looked up and said, "I am?"

Santa was enthusiastic. "Sure!," he said.

Santa gave him the present provided by his mother. The boy was so weak he could barely open the wrapping paper. When he saw what was inside, he flashed a big smile and laid his head back down.

"They say I'm gonna die," the boy said. "How can I tell when I get to where I'm going?"

Santa didn't break his jolly composure. "Can you do me a big favor?," he asked.

"Sure!," the boy said, perking up.

"When you get there, you tell 'em you're Santa's Number One elf, and I know they'll let you in." It was as if Santa was letting him in on an inside secret.

The boy said, "They will?"

Santa beamed, "Sure!"

The boy pushed up and gave Santa a big hug, but he had one more request. "Santa, can you help me?"

Santa wrapped his arms around the boy. Before the boy could say anything, he died. Santa just kept hugging him.

Everyone outside the room realized what happened. His mother ran in. She was screaming, "No, no, not yet!" Santa handed her son back and went home without a word.

It's a moving, tear-jerking, beautiful story, right? It also might be completely fabricated.[239] Apart from the account given by the man who played Santa and a few text messages around the alleged encounter, no hospital staff were ever able to corroborate the story. The Santa actor refused to identify the family of the boy, citing privacy concerns. Still, the local news story went viral on the internet, and was uncritically reprinted in a dozen major media outlets across the globe before its reliability was seriously questioned.

Perhaps you've read much of this book and you've been pleasantly surprised. Maybe even to your chagrin, the Christian faith that has been presented on these pages is not

---

[239] Emanuella Grinberg, "Tale of Boy Who Died in Santa's Arms Unravels" CNN, https://www.cnn.com/2016/12/14/us/knoxville-santa-story-in-question-trnd/.

like the Christianity you've seen featured in the media or from that obnoxious Christian friend or family member. Not only does Christianity seem potentially like a force for great good in your life and the world, it at times seems…beautiful. If this is really the Christian faith, who *wouldn't* want to trust in this story of faith, hope, and love?

Then again, it might also be a fabrication. If not fabricated, perhaps the well-intentioned wishes of people trying to reform religion into something gentler and more benevolent. Like some of the more skeptical ancient Greek philosophers, they knew all along that these stories weren't real, but were just working with the best myths available to them to help make the world a better place.[240] Even today, some extremely liberal clergy fall into this category. The story of the Christian faith may be beautiful, but perhaps only as a feel-good story that insulates us from the crushing despair that can come with atheism and meaninglessness.

As we consider how to respond to the story of faith, hope, and love bound up in relationship with the Triune God, I want to offer caution in understanding beauty this way. Just as I mentioned earlier that physical or aesthetic beauty is not the kind of beauty we are seeking, we are not supposed to look to beauty as solely a buffer against existential ugliness. This reduces beauty to an utilitarian function, and truth judged solely by its utility is unlikely to be truth.

So, if beauty draws us into something that is not true, we do ourselves no favors by patronizing it with civil remarks and flattery. It is beauty in service to a lie. It is caked-on makeup and too much booze at last call. Jesus called this kind of beauty, "whitewashed tombs" – painted and clean on the outside, but covering up the rotting corpses within.[241]

---

[240] Plato, *Republic*, 383, 415c6-5.
[241] Matthew 23:27

Responding Not to a What, But a Who

The late critic of monotheistic religions, Christopher Hitchens, once said, "We keep on being told that religion, whatever its imperfections, at least instills morality. On every side, there is conclusive evidence that the contrary is the case and that faith causes people to be more mean, more selfish, and perhaps above all, more stupid."[242] Hitchens made it one of his life's missions to shame people out of respecting religious belief, whether that was Christianity, Judaism, or Islam.

You might be surprised to know that I tend to agree with my neo-atheist friends here, the devotees of Christopher Hitchens, Richard Dawkins, Sam Harris, and the like. We should not give special deference to religious values or institutions if we are convinced that they are based on beliefs that are simply not true, and even more so if we perceive those beliefs as leading to harm. To do so would honor superstition and ignorance, and the world already has enough of both.

Some commentators have criticized these "evangelical" atheists as being too caustic and intolerant, but I believe my neo-atheist friends are doing a great service to the Christian faith. Currently, it is culturally fashionable not to explicitly reject the gospel, but rather to coyly avoid responding to Christ's invitation. And yet implicit in the momentous nature of a marriage proposal is the demand for a "yes" or a "no" response. Jesus Christ was very gracious in his teachings, but he never seemed to let anyone he encountered off the proverbial hook. He is recorded saying in three separate gospel accounts, "Whoever does not take his cross and follow me is not worthy of me. Whoever finds his life will lose it, and whoever loses his life for my sake will find it."[243]

---

[242] Lee Moller, *The God Con: Pay, Pray, Obey* (Victoria, BC: Friesen Press, 2017), 213.
[243] Matthew 16:24-25; Mark 8:34-35; Luke 9:23-24

You either followed him or watched him pass by. You either obeyed him or ignored his commands. You either worshiped him as the Son of God or called him a liar or a madman.

Our polite society doesn't like being forced to respond this clearly. This kind of clarity is so uncomfortable for us that we instead choose to pacify the situation with platitudes about Jesus. We call him a "'good teacher of the golden rule," an "enlightened being," or even a "messenger from God."

This attempt at flattery, however, is a social sleight of hand, a rhetorical ruse designed to make us feel less awkward. These so-called compliments about Jesus are actually backhanded insults, because they all claim a perception of Jesus that Jesus himself specifically did not allow. Time and time again Jesus rejected attempts to placate him with compliments that were inconsistent with his claims to divinity and God's mission to rescue and redeem the world. Jesus even implied that cursing him is a more appropriate response.[244] Some may find that disrespectful of religion or God, but I think that it is to miss the point. Jesus doesn't care about whether someone is respectful of generalized religion or some sanitized concept of the divine; he cares about your response to him.

The story of the life, death, and resurrection of Jesus demands a response, "yes" or "no." Like a marriage proposal, a "maybe" is an effectual "no."

To be clear, we do not say "yes" or "no" to the beauty of the story. No story, no matter how beautifully woven, can move our souls from estrangement to reconciliation. This is inherently and exclusively a relational process. Our response is not to an impersonal "what," but our personal "who." Our response is to Christ.

---

[244] Revelation 3:15

This also means that to respond to the invitation of Christ is not blind faith, a naive and drunken saunter into "the sweet by-and-by." Rather, the beauty of the Christian faith is akin to a radiant engagement ring offered up on bended knee by the Creator of the universe. Understood this way, faith is not blind or a one-time decision, but neither is it cynically demanding of constant evidence. The faith of the Christian is meant to be relational as any other part of the gospel. It is meant to model the road to marriage.

When two people meet for the first time, even if there is great physical and emotional attraction, only the most reckless people would propose marriage on the spot. You simply can't know the character of a stranger to warrant giving your life to them. Dating, in its various cultural expressions, is designed in part to determine the trustworthiness of a potential spouse. The declaration of "I love you" on a first date means very little. That same vow at the wedding altar means everything.

The same should be true for anyone considering the claims of Christianity. If the invitation of Christ is nothing less than a proposal of eternal marriage with the Triune God, this should not be accepted lightly. Jesus is not asking to be your boyfriend. Our response needs to critically and logically examine the trustworthiness of the invitation.

How do you do this? There are typically three reasons why we are hesitant to accept Christ's invitation to be in relationship with him. These reasons could be summarized as doubt, pride, and fear. Sometimes these are difficult to recognize, especially within ourselves, so it's important that we develop the self-awareness of where those hesitations are in our own lives.

The Hesitation of Doubt

Perhaps most obvious is doubt, or an intellectual hesitation. You have unanswered questions about the reliability of the Scriptures, or the resurrection, or some burning dilemma that makes it impossible for you to embrace the story of faith, hope, and love.

Personally, I think this is the easiest hesitation to resolve. There are volumes of books by brilliant theologians, historians, and scientists dedicated to answering the issues that the Christian faith stands or falls on. For anyone willing to put in the work, the intellectual hesitations often resolve themselves in short order. I have also observed that many people often find that their particular hesitation, while not unimportant, is not actually crucial to making a reasonable response to the heart of Christ's invitation. You don't need to know *everything* about a potential spouse before getting married, and even after there will always be *some* mystery in the relationship.

This may surprise you, but I have never met a person whose rejection of Christ was based solely on intellectual objections. In fact, I have never met any skeptic who truly tried to resolve their academic questions around Christianity and was unable to overcome their doubts.

Please don't take this as dismissiveness. People who are *only* vexed by intellectual objections despite a sincere desire to believe certainly exist, but in all probability you're not one of them. It's not that skeptics don't have worthwhile intellectual concerns about following a resurrected rabbi from the first century – they absolutely do and *should*. It's that without exception, I have found that the hesitation in the driver's seat came from a place more recessed in their hearts.

The Hesitation of Pride

Far more often, the hesitations come from a love of something they thought was more satisfying than relationship with God. Running the calculus, it was clear that to receive Christ into their life meant needing to jettison less worthy affections.

It is often a love for the sins that have consciously or subconsciously served as the balm for our lingering existential dread and our insecurity about our worthiness to be accepted and loved by our peers. Sometimes these sins are unhealthy and we know they are unhealthy, but we like them all the same. Other times, they are noble affections like work, family, or relationships that we have elevated to the most important and controlling affection of our lives. Either way, they function as conceptual idols, functional saviors that we think will make us happy, or at least help us to stay afloat in our increasingly desperate dogpaddle through a sea of despair.

To make this change though requires repentance, which means a turning in the opposite direction. Repentance requires humility and our pride objects loudly. Whether it is the sins we love too much or our willingness to confess them, either may be too embarrassing to admit to ourselves or others. Instead, our pride suggests we cover these hesitations up with more respectable "intellectual objections" to the Christian faith. *It's not that I love my sin too much,* I tell myself, *it's that I'm a logical, freethinking person who knows better than to fall for religious myths.*

To be honest, this hesitation of pride can be extremely difficult to root out. Apart from perhaps the penetrating insight from a trusted friend who is also a Christian, I do not know of a helpful solution. For example, if you suffer from this kind of hesitation, your pride fights back within you even as you read these words, shouting *that's not me!* The nature of pride can't even acknowledge its own capabilities of self-sabotage.

Fortunately, pride has a hard time keeping its guard up twenty-four hours a day, seven days a week. Like a moment of clarity for an addict after a binge, there are fleeting but merciful windows of awareness where we realize that our unwillingness to exchange our love of sin for the love of God is the major motivation behind our other so-called objections to the Christian faith. If we are to recognize a hesitation that comes from pride, we must be willing to see the dark moments of self-doubt as, in fact, divine mercies.

The Hesitation of Fear

It would be unfair to say all objections to the Christian faith are simply red herrings to cover up our pride about our sin. There is one other hesitation that may exist within you, and that is fear. Unlike doubt and pride, fear does not push us away from Christ's invitation with an emphatic "no," but with a hesitant "maybe."

As we explored earlier, to be human is to experience anxiety. Even fiancés madly in love feel some anxiety as their wedding day looms closer. Fear is the consolidated power of multiple anxieties, and it paralyzes our ability to decide or take action. It is possible that between some minor lingering intellectual hesitations and a handful of relatively meager sins that you think you need to hold on to, these have combined with anxiety about an unknown future to freeze your heart in fear. When faced with Christ's invitation, "what ifs" large and small flash before you.

- *What if by embracing the Christian faith, I'm signing up to check my brain at the church door?*

- *What if I'll be pressured to believe things I don't know if I really agree with?*
- *What if I'll be pressured to conform to an ethic I don't know if I really want to practice?*
- *What if I'll be condemned by other Christians if I don't?*
- *What if I really do give up all the things that I value more than God, and God doesn't really come through?*
- *What if becoming a Christian will only make my life worse in the end?*

Anxiety can snowball into fear quicker and with more subtlety than we might imagine. Once fear has gripped us, our response is to retreat to a holding pattern that mitigates our sense of danger. For the person considering Christ's invitation, they may suddenly find themselves finding reasons to not attend church or Christian gatherings as a way to subconsciously dodge the need to respond to God. That same person may start asking for more academic resources on obscure details of the Christian faith, as if they cannot respond to God until they can resolve some secondary issue that is something clearly other than the gospel itself. They may even plunge themselves headlong back into their sins or functional saviors, trying them one more time to see if they might bring the satisfaction or purpose that God claims to exclusively offer.

If you feel like you are suffering from the hesitation of fear, know that you are in good company. From C.S. Lewis to Saint Augustine to the patriarch Abraham, all experienced the grip of fear before yielding to the invitation of God. Even better than the company we share, the good news that existed for them also exists for you. God doesn't demand unwavering belief from us, brazenly free from the fear of the unknown. We are only asked to trust, and let God prove Godself faithful to us.

There is a story about Jesus' ministry where a desperate father pleads with him to heal his son of a horrendously violent demonic force that has possessed him for years. However, the father, likely disappointed by just as many years of empty religious platitudes and failed solutions that have brought his son no relief, confesses his doubts that Jesus can do any better. He's heard enough though about this Jesus that makes him think it's worth an attempt.

The father cries out, "I believe, help my unbelief!"

Jesus' response would have shocked his first-century audience. He does not condemn him for his lack of spiritual devotion. He does not tell him to go back to the local synagogue and work on his faith until he can muster up some super-spiritual belief. The father's meager faith – full of whatever mixture of skepticism, pride, and fear – is sufficient. Jesus heals his son of the demonic force.[245]

God uses our small steps of trust to authenticate God's great trustworthiness. God takes even our anxious faith, and calms it with a peace that passes understanding.[246]

Whether you are struggling with skepticism, pride, or fear to Christ's invitation, the resolution is found in the minor, but consistent steps of trust. That quick prayer you didn't think was reverent-sounding enough. The visit to a church Sunday morning when you're still a little hung over and don't know the words to the songs. Reading a chapter from the Bible even when you can't pronounce half the names in it and understand the story even less. Even if you feel like you're doing it "wrong," don't stop trying. God knows your heart. God will respond.

We are not asked to take an absurd leap of faith into the unknown, but neither are we meant to ask God for a string of divine signs. We may feel mysteriously prompted to do the former, or graciously given the latter, but neither is required

---

[245] For the entire story, read Mark 9:14-29
[246] Romans 4:20; Philippians 4:6-7

from us or from God. Like a burgeoning romance, we only need to take the next step of faith, and in doing so, we open ourselves to experiencing the goodness of gospel and relationship with Christ.

The Same Choice All Over Again

It is ironic then, or perhaps poetic, that we have come full circle to our primordial ancestors.

Thousands of years later, the dilemma of Adam and Eve is also your dilemma. Faced with the inescapable uncertainty of our lives, we too experience the universal human emotion of anxiety. No different than Adam and Eve, you too are faced with the same two choices that hung before them, trust or distrust of God's love and provision for us. Every generation has faced it. To some degree, every human who has ever lived has faced it. It is a choice older than history itself.

Crippling fear, blinding pride, callous cynicism – all these things are the almost instantaneous byproduct of distrust. In choosing not to trust God, our primordial ancestors succumbed to sin, and we have been beset by its abusive spell ever since.

Even now, in each human life, God desires to start anew, to break the cycle. Christ has broken the power of sin that we might break our addiction to it, to live and think and love freely, basking in the grace of God. Addiction is rarely overcome by substituting other drugs, even rarer still by our own willpower. Instead we find that addiction, even to some of the world's hardest drugs, is overcome by feeling truly loved and cared for.

Christ is the spouse and Christ's Church is the family that speaks to our inner hearts – past every reason to keep God at arms' length – to let this divine love and care into our spirit. When we do, God is faithful to begin the healing process. Our condition, perceptibly but also imperceptibly, begins to change. Our justification by Christ yoked together with our sanctification under Christ leads us into what Christians across the ages have said makes life sublimely joyful: *union with Christ.*

To experience union with Christ is to have the streams of Eden spring up in our veins. God begins to walk with us again in the cool breeze of our prayers. We move forward to an eternal destiny even as we are carried back before the dawn of time.

Yet remember, this is not merely a matter of personal benefit. We cannot be spiritual mercenaries seeking internal or eternal bliss, as wonderful as that is. God doesn't just love you. God loves your neighbor too. And your enemy.

To accept Christ's intimate invitation to restore your heart is to accept Christ's revolutionary command to help God in restoring the world. Not a day goes by where the world does not desperately need it. Not a day goes by where the faithfulness of a Christian following in the way of Jesus does not contribute to it. The world's condition, perceptibly but also imperceptibly, begins to change.

You see, your choice to trust or distrust God all over again is far grander than you ever imagined. Reconciliation from estrangement is far more cosmic than we are ever able to entertain. It has everything to do with you and your future. It also has everything to do with the world and its future. It is personal, yet anything but private. You are never choosing for just yourself. The whole of creation awaits your choice.

Still, somehow, the weight of the world is not on our shoulders. That weight was already borne on a cross.

The strange, but beautiful paradox is still true. Nothing is required of us. Everything has already been done for you.

All that remains is your response.

GLOSSARY OF TERMS

CHAPTER ONE The Wager

FAITH
　　Relational trust based on prior authentication and evidence.
DISCIPLES
　　"Students," in reference to Jesus' students.
APOSTLES
　　"Messengers," in reference to Jesus' disciples after his resurrection, and leaders of the first church.
SAINT PETER
　　An inner-circle disciple of Jesus and founder of the church in Jerusalem. He is credited with writing 1st Peter, 2nd Peter, and primary source material for the Gospel of Mark before he was executed.

CHAPTER TWO The Measure

SAINT PAUL
　　A former persecutor of Christians who founded at least 14 first-century churches and wrote approximately 25% of the New Testament before he was executed.
OLD TESTAMENT
　　39 (Protestant) or 46 (Roman Catholic) or 49 (Greek Orthodox) biblical books written before the life of Jesus.
NEW TESTAMENT
　　27 biblical books written after the life of Jesus.
CANONIZATION
　　The process of consensus by which the Church recognized spiritual texts as authoritative for Christian belief and practice.
AUTHORITATIVE
　　In reference to the belief that the Bible is the most reliable witness to work and will of God in the world, requiring submission after a process of faithful interpretation.

CHAPTER THREE Love Through Creation

SAINT JOHN

An inner-circle disciple of Jesus and a leader of the church in Jerusalem and Ephesus. He is credited with writing the Gospel of John, 1st, 2nd, and 3rd John, and Revelation.

CREATIO EX NIHILIO

"Creation from nothing," in reference to God's making of the universe.

EARLY CHURCH

Commonly marked as the era of Christianity before it was legalized in 313 CE.

TRINITY

The description of God as a single being that is comprised of three personas or persons coexisting in perfect unity.

TRANSCENDANT

Existing outside of space-time and in reference to the Creator / Father of the Trinity.

INCARNATIONAL

Existing in human form and in reference to the Redeemer / Son of the Trinity.

IMMANENT

Existing inside of space-time and in reference to the Sustainer / Holy Spirit of the Trinity.

PERICHORESIS

"Circle dance," in reference to an ancient metaphor of the Trinity being like a flowing dance.

IMAGO DEI

"Image of God," in reference to the divine nature bestowed by God to every human.

SOVEREIGN

In reference to God's ultimate power over all existence, including human affairs. God's sovereignty, however, does not necessitate micromanaging of nature or humanity.

OMNISCIENT

"All-Knowing," in reference to a key attribute of God. Outside of time, God is aware of all moments that are past, present, or future to those within time.

OMNIPOTENT

"All-Powerful," in reference to a key attribute of God. God can do anything logically possible within God's self-described nature and character.

ADAM

"Humanity," in reference to some early male humans before recorded history.

EVE

"Source of Life," in reference to some early female humans before recorded history.

EDEN

A walled garden where some early humans resided, represented by Adam and Eve, and lived in harmonious relationship with one another and with God.

CHAPTER FOUR Faith In The Past

Act I: Betrayal

TREE OF LIFE

A tree in Eden passed over by Adam and Eve for the tree forbidden by God.

THE SATAN

"The Adversary, the Accuser," in reference to the force that opposes the will and love of God.

THE FALL

The event where the humans that God had created harmonious relationship with, chose to distrust God and became estranged from God, ushering in seemingly irreversible destructive consequences.

SIN

Fundamentally a distrust of either God's goodness or sovereignty, leading to suffering and destruction.

Act II: Pursuit

PROTO-GOSPEL
> "First-good news," in reference to stories in the Old Testament that foreshadow in incarnation, death, and resurrection of Jesus

COVENANT
> A solemn agreement, in reference to God initiating a series contractual promises with God's creation.

ABRAHAMIC COVENANT
> The most thematically important covenant in the Bible, where God promises to bless all people of the earth through a single person.

PEOPLE OF THE COVENANT
> A community directly engaged by God's grace, first in reference to the Hebrew people and now also applied to Christian communities.

PROPHET
> A messenger who calls people back to covenantal faithfulness.

TYPOLOGY
> A symbolic action or person that is later repeated in another action or person, namely that of Jesus.

Act III: Reconciliation

INCARNATION OF GOD
> God the Son, the Redeemer, being born as a human.

JESUS OF NAZARETH
> The most direct name of Jesus that was likely used during his ministry.

SON OF GOD
> A title of Jesus given by his followers and announced from Heaven, which reflected his divine nature and a rejection of Roman emperor worship.

SON OF MAN
> Jesus' title for himself that reflected his divine solidarity with humanity.

THE NICENE CREED
> The first formal statement of beliefs by the Church published in the 4th century.

VIRGIN BIRTH

The doctrine that Jesus was miraculously conceived without human sperm in a rare medical phenomenon known as parthenogenesis.

EVANGELION

"Good news" delivered on behalf of a victorious general or liberating king.

"I AM"

One of the holiest names for the Hebrew monotheistic God, recorded in the Gospel of John as used by Jesus to explicitly and implicitly describe himself.

EUCHARIST/LORD'S SUPPER/HOLY COMMUNION

One of the two universal Christian sacraments, where the wine is spiritually or symbolically understood as the blood of Christ, and the bread the body of Christ.

BAPTISM

One of the two universal Christian sacraments. which is meant to picture a public identification with Jesus and the power of Christ to remove sin.

RESURRECTION

More than a resuscitation from death, this refers to someone who is dead returning to life in a condition of immortality.

THE ASCENSION

Jesus transmitting himself from our earthly dimension to the dimension of Heaven 40 days after his resurrection.

CHAPTER FIVE Love From Heaven

THE NEW ADAM

A title given to Jesus by Saint Paul, referring to the understanding that where the first humans sinned by distrusting God and unleashing sin into the world, Jesus would remain sinless by trusting God and ultimately reversing the power of sin in the world.

ATONEMENT

The means by which God reconciles the estranged humanity and creates harmony. The Christian faith has multiple, complementary theories of how God primarily achieved this.

RANSOM THEORY

Jesus Christ atones for humanity by rescuing humanity from Satan's control and bringing us back to God.

CHRISTUS VICTOR THEORY

Jesus Christ atones for humanity by defeating the powers of evil and firmly establishing the Kingdom of God.

SATISFACTION THEORY

Jesus Christ atones for humanity by paying our spiritual debt to God or enduring the divine justice that was meant for us because of our sin, canceling our debt and declaring us innocent before God.

RECAPITULATION THEORY

Jesus Christ atones for humanity by entering into death and corruption in order to reverse the effects of sin, ultimately becoming the healing cure for all that sin touches.

JUSTIFICATION

The condition of being accepted and embraced by God, enabled by Jesus Christ's atoning work.

SANCTIFICATION

The gradual process of conforming one's life to the will and love God in light of being justified before God.

THEODICY

Making sense of the nature of God alongside the existence of evil and suffering.

THE WAY

The earliest name for worshipers of Jesus Christ.

CHAPTER SIX Hope In The Future

SECOND COMING

The return of Jesus Christ to defeat all evil, judge humanity, merge Heaven and Earth, and consummate the union of Christ and his people.

ESCHATOLOGY

"Study of last things," in reference to the Second Coming and its composite events.

HEAVEN

Eternal union with the Triune God through the marriage of Christ and his reconciled people.

HELL

Total estrangement from the Triune God.

CHAPTER SEVEN Love For The World

NOW-AND-NOT-YET

Referring to the tension between the observation that the Kingdom of God has irrevocably established itself on Earth, but has not yet completely displaced evil and effects of estrangement.

THE KINGDOM OF GOD

Anywhere the will and love of God is lived out.

THE CHURCH

People called by God to worship Christ and demonstrate the Kingdom of God to the world.

THE GREAT COMMISSION

The mandate given by Jesus Christ for the Church to make disciples in the way of Jesus' teachings.

CONFESSING CHURCHES

Churches that have, at different times in history, refused the government's demands to abandon fundamental tenets of the Christian faith, usually at the cost of imprisonment, torture, or death.

CHAPTER EIGHT The Response

UNION WITH CHRIST

Referring to the synchronistic effects of our justification and sanctification, enabling spiritual intimacy and joy with Christ as our faith progresses in life.

ABOUT THE AUTHOR

Colin Kerr (M.Div) is the founding pastor of Parkside Church and an ordained minister in the Presbyterian Church (U.S.A.). He previously spent eight years assisting historic congregations with church renewal strategies and planting a new multi-campus college ministry, which grew to become one of the largest Presbyterian collegiate ministries in the nation. Colin and his family live in Charleston, South Carolina. He can be reached at rev.colin.kerr@gmail.com.

Made in United States
Orlando, FL
25 April 2022

17183238R00126